# Communicating
# When Your Company
# Is Under Siege

# Communicating
# When Your Company
# Is Under Siege
## Surviving Public Crisis

*by*

MARION K. PINSDORF

Lexington Books

*D.C. Heath and Company* • *Lexington, Massachusetts* • *Toronto*

*Library of Congress Cataloging-in-Publication Data*

Pinsdorf, Marion K.
Communicating when your company is under siege.

Bibliography: p.
Includes index.
1. Corporate image.   2.   Public relations.
3. Crisis management.   4.   Communication in
management.   5.   Strategic planning.   I.   Title.
HD59.2.P55     1987          659.2          85–45473
ISBN 0–669–11790–0 (alk. paper)

Published simultaneously in Canada
Printed in the United States of America
Casebound International Standard Book Number: 0–669–11790–0
Library of Congress Catalog Card Number: 85–45473

The paper used in this publication meets
the minimum requirements of American National Standard
for Information Sciences – Permanence of Paper
for Printed Library Materials, ANSI Z39.48–1984

ISBN 0-669-11790-0

86 87 88 89 90 8 7 6 5 4 3 2 1

*Dedicated to*
*two chief executive officers,*
*pragmatists who communicated*
*with candor and conviction:*
*Henry A. Walker, Jr.,*
*Amfac, Inc.*
*and*
*the late John W. Hill,*
*Hill and Knowlton, Inc.*

# Contents

# Preface/Memo

To:      CEO and Senior Operating Officers

From:    Marion K. Pinsdorf

Subject: Communicating During Corporate Troubles

---

Besieged as you are by the production breakdowns, stiffer Japanese competition, and just plain keeping our company profitable during the current economic retrenchment and downturn, corporate communications may seem soft and ancillary—draining profits rather than producing them.

Communications is soft, all right: the soft underbelly of our business, vulnerable to losses not only of money, but of that ephemeral yet important public perception. Many companies (but fortunately not *yet* ours) have been pounded by expensive events that came winging in from the outside. Think what Tylenol cost Johnson & Johnson, and that crisis was a public success in 1982. Or Bhopal, Union Carbide. Or the Pentagon's charges against General Dynamics. Or even that relatively simple explosion at our competitor's plant. Granted, how well we respond to such challenges depends largely on how strong and profitable we are internally, but we need to recognize and plan for external crises, particularly those that erupt without warning.

Maladroit communications can create and deepen many corporate calamities—destroy markets, financial strength, and reputations; cost a company its existence and you your job; and then leave in its wake protracted investigations and expensive fines. Millions are spent on advertising, product liability, and legal fees, but only a few cents—and even less executive time—on perception liability or public damage control. When E.F. Hutton speaks now, the SEC listens, not its customers. Had Hutton understood a cardinal rule of communications—there are no secrets—they might have been flourishing instead of sullied. We can learn how to survive from such very expensive communications crises of others.

You all have as many good reasons as would-be dieters for not developing a communications strategy. A few compelling arguments, which will become clear, dictate the contrary. First, in an age when we depend on machines to do our thinking and attempt to quantify everything, it's hard to measure communications, which seldom can produce numbers to prove its contribution and utility. And how those public relations types go on and on when they have a case that does.

Then there's the department itself. Too often it's used as the dumping ground for corporate losers, burn-outs awaiting retirement, or ill-trained, unfocused but bright liberal arts graduates. They are consigned to communications, where supposedly they can do less harm than if they were running a plant. High schools put football coaches and driver education teachers in history departments with the same rationale. Oh yes, it's also been the corporate EEO token, where women and blacks get their first shots at senior management.

The communications officer carries these stigmata as well as the burden of being a Janus manager—charged with knowing our business well, but also scanning the world outside for elements, hostile or advantageous, which influence our operations. It's a damn delicate role to caution about dangerous specks on the competitive horizon or to warn that you are being carried away by your enthusiasm for that pending merger. Often the communications officer is thrust into the uncomfortable role of corporate conscience, pointing out how much cost overruns on government contracts or a polluted stream are going to cost, not just in good will but in dollars—lots of them. We are all more civilized than the Greeks, who simply beheaded a bearer of bad news; instead, we tune him out, relegate him to impotency, or, if he's too persistent, fire him.

And he must cope daily with your *bête noire*—the media. When you are immersed in problems, nothing annoys you more than the press emphasizing the negative or searching out the sensational, not behaving as corporate types do, or exercising news judgment very different from yours. Some of these adversarial relations are understandable: your aims are often different. But well trained, good reporters do share your goal of honestly telling your corporate story to the public. Should a headline or television news segment be unfair or damaging, however, it's the communications officer who must bring it to you and explain. Too often he's blamed for whatever the reporter wrote.

The most effective, even profitable communications is embedded in the matrix of our business and the general economic, social milieu, not positioned atop Mt. Olympus as a staff function. Communications can counter the wishful thinking so endemic today: that somehow next year will be much better than the dismal one just past. Communications can be a valuable correcting device, a very loyal, questioning devil's advocate. And it keeps shaking your shoulder, telling you to look out the window at a wider world. The rest of us are just too pressured with the details of running the business to do this, although we all know we should.

All of us who have awakened in anguish at 3 A.M. because of the crunch of corporate pressures smile at the panacea peddlers with their simple nostrums and one-minute easy how-to-dos—entertaining corporate fairy tales. We know the reality is much tougher, but also gives a much deeper sense of accomplishment.

Read on if you want to think and to pick my thoughts, which have been trained in journalism and history, then battle-tested in the trenches of communications counseling and senior corporate management.

# Acknowledgments

POLYNESIANS customarily thank everyone. When distilling a lifetime of thought and professional experience in a field as everchanging as communications, it is difficult to do otherwise.

Did the learning start with demanding historians—professors Robert Brunhouse of Drew University, John Fagg of New York University, and Carl Bridenbaugh of Brown University—who kept me constantly searching for the biases—intentional or unconscious—in the fabric of writing and decision-making? Or the psychologists—professors James A. McClintock of Drew and Ferdinand Jones of Brown—who heightened my understanding of how vulnerable and noble leaders can be?

But before the educators was journalism. One editor, infected with "Front Page" style, profanely bellowed every mistake and stupidity of a scared sixteen-year-old across the city room. The late Pulitzer Prize winner William A. Caldwell taught us journalists to think widely and deeply, even on the police beat.

Coming into communications in the 1960s, I was fortunate to learn from two pioneers in corporate communications and in counseling: Milton Fairman of Borden Inc. taught with all the cussedness of his early Chicago newspaper days, and John W. Hill, founder of Hill and Knowlton, Inc., with indefatigable curiosity and collegiality. The bridge from counseling to corporate officer was crossed with the encouragement of Edward Starr, retired Hill and Knowlton executive vice president, and Henry A. Walker Jr., CEO, now chairman of Amfac, Inc., who has the unique gifts of listening sensitively, implementing swiftly, and appreciating worlds much wider than many business executives.

As a corporate officer myself, I learned from the chairmen I served: the impact of high national visibility from G. William Miller and Robert P.

Straetz of Textron; the quicksand of merger from Ralph A. Saul of INA (now CIGNA) the practicality of Japanese ideas from Henry Wendt of Smithkline Beckman; the importance of Brazil from Augustine R. Marusi of Borden; the wisdom and productivity of participatory decision-making from Sidney Harman of Harman International; and the wisdom and patience of Portuguese traditions from Nelson Vieira, Director of Brown University's Center for Portuguese and Brazilian studies, where I have taught for seven years.

During the best of corporate times and the worst, an intelligent, compassionate circle of confidants have cared. Their titles and accomplishments are impressive, but their greatest gift to me has been their friendship over many years, miles, and job changes, through successes and pain. They are: Robert Ames, James Baar, Chester Burger, Robert L. Dilenschneider, William Ford, Robert K. Gray, Bert Heffner, John Leo, Ellen Magnin Newman, Daniel Picard, Albert Ross, and Larry M. Speakes.

And the personal friends: Joan and Martin Ainbinder, Nessa Forman, Jud and Helen Goldsmith, Edgar and Beatrice Buckler Gotthold, Roberta Jacobs, Zoltán and Clarissa Kiss, Patricia C. Kroepke, Roy Schantz, Barbara Shelby-Merello, Marian E. Shelby, and Lily G. Spierer. And to my Amfac colleagues, directors, and officers, who translate *aloha* as supporting and enthusing.

Leonia is a special little town, long ago dedicated to artistic and creative achievement. You work with the sense of the outstanding people who once made their homes there. Some years ago, two then neighbors, Bob and Mary Ludlum, encouraged my dreams of writing. Edward Brewer at his harpsichord took the lonely edge off writing. And Sushil and Veena Chadda, Harriet Maneval, and Barbara Leonowicz were always caring. Harold Ficke, director of the public library, and his staff found any book I needed.

All these people are both prologue to this book and very much a part of it. My specific thanks are extended to Dave Dyer, then associate editor of the *Harvard Business Review*, who started it all by introducing me to Bruce Katz, who became a supportive, sensitive editor and friend. And to the people who shared ideas and experiences generously: Karen Berg of Commcore; Chester Burger and Alfred Geduldig of Chester Burger and Company; Harold Burson of Burson Marsteller; Richard Cheney, Richard Hyde, and Robert Taft of Hill and Knowlton; William Dobbins of Reliance Group Holdings; Phillip Fried of Monsanto; Kirk O. Hanson of Stanford Business School; Harry Matte and Robert Ozaki of Amfac; Allan E. Shubert of *Fortune*; Michael Tabriz of Philip Morris; and many others over the years who thought analytically about communications.

From each I have learned that the fun and accomplishment of a career comes not on a mill pond, but in surviving the waves and troughs of turbulent waters. To each, *mahalo*.

# Communicating
# When Your Company
# Is Under Siege

# 1

# Turbulent Times

## *The Kaleidoscope of Corporate Communications*

C ORPORATE communications is a kaleidoscope of everchanging functions, talents, and crises that do not so much proceed as crystallize anew each time. With each turn, each event or crisis, a different configuration forms. What worked previously helps in understanding the new cluster, but, in truth, each serious public crisis is different. Tunnel vision—looking down the tube at the kaleidoscope's always changing colors—reveals only surface happenings at a given moment, not the lingering shadows of events long drained of their power or the shifting elements that may presage the future. Communications decisions, often solidly rooted in quicksand, as a result pose greater-than-usual challenges and risks to operating executives—who must depend upon and evaluate the function—and, most of all, to the communicators themselves.

To be effective—or of any use at all—communications must be intimately, intelligently interwoven with the sobering realities of the times and the business it seeks to serve. It cannot be a cosmetic attempt to gussy up ugly or dishonest facts with a false, pretty face. Realities in the mid-1980s mean understanding shrinking rather than expanding markets, and demassing the economy and some of the elephantine corporate structures that no longer function effectively and profitably. Managers must motivate a new breed of employees: less loyal, and more demanding and impatient; seeking more individualism; gathering information from sight, sound, and each other more than from traditional print sources; and stuck below what they were taught to expect.

Companies must face tougher off-shore competition. Some warn the United States is in danger of becoming a service island in a manufacturing world, of putting very educated people to work slinging Big Macs—for life. Often overlooked is the penchant for naiveté and wastefulness. A military example illustrates a corporate problem. Tom Mangold and John Penycate, writing on the Vietnam War, describe how well Americans lived above the Tunnels of CuChi and how poorly the Vietnamese existed below. But the obvious disadvantages to the Viet Cong were balanced. The Americans used large numbers of support soldiers and fighters, required many supplies, and were hobbled because every night they returned to base. They were hobbled, too, by retrieving their wounded. Underneath, the Vietnamese listened, fought, and supplied themselves on U.S. leftovers and discarded food and arms. In stark contrast to regular troops, Americans who eventually became tunnel rats themselves were very cool, calculating, and careful with their supplies and opportunities.

Corporate changes are swift and unforgiving. Many examples could be chosen, but the decline of Chesebrough-Pond's will illustrate. Heralded just a few years ago by *In Search of Excellence*, as one of the best managed U.S. companies, its growth quickly turned anemic. The company was plagued by rapid management turnover, maturing markets, a dearth of new products, and excessive debt. Like many managements today, Chesebrough-Pond preferred buying products to growing them. Polaroid let good practices grow undisciplined. Guaranteed employment mutated into a civil service attitude of sinecure. Once innovative employees became overpaid and undermotivated, with little understanding of Polaroid's long-term goals or, more importantly, its changed competitive climate.

A poignant picture of change can be found in the two portrayals of Willy Loman in Arthur Miller's *Death of a Salesman*. In the 1950s Lee J. Cobb played a big, bluff salesman huckstering American goods for hungry markets. He dreamed big, failed tragically. In the mid-1980s, Dustin Hoffman played Willy as a shuffling shrimp who started smaller than Cobb and ended up defeated even in modest aspirations. Instead of buoyant expansion, he was, as one reviewer noted, "The graduate who can't even make a killing in plastics."

Once all institutions were perceived—incorrectly, even in boom times—as everlasting, always expanding, and supportive. Now, as Peter Drucker points out, they are brittle and staid; they must limber up. Comparisons of the top 100 companies fifty years ago with those today document just how brittle companies are under the press of changing technology, markets, and competition. A survey by Patrick-Douglas Outplacement in Cleveland reports that about one quarter of the CEOs in *Fortune* 500 companies were replaced between 1983 and 1985, about forty-one percent of financial chiefs, and about twenty-seven percent of human resources officers. They don't keep count of communications chiefs, but you could guess that their turnover rate would be very high. Loyalty has been sundered up—even with golden parachutes—and down. V.R. Buzzotta, writing in *The New York Times* points out that twenty-three percent of the nation's 850 leading corporations underwent "operational restructuring" in the first three quarters of 1985—buying, selling, or consolidating businesses. These moves directly affected about 1.3 million workers. About a half million management jobs have been lost since 1979, most of them in the wake of a merger or a related change. As a result, employee morale and support have declined substantially, according to Buzzotta—most dramatically and seriously among managers.[1]

## Communicating on Consent of Constituencies

With all the imperative business and personnel problems, it is all too easy for the pressured executive to consign communications to the back burner. But this book will demonstrate that such relegation is done at great peril and expense. Trace lines of concern are apparent to academics and businessmen alike. George Cabot Lodge of Harvard Business School writes of companies being able (even allowed) to operate in the future only by consent of their constituencies—a commercial application of Lockean theories of government by consent of the governed. Rafael D. Pagan, Jr., president of the Nestlé Coordination Center for Nutrition, says flatly that activists have done a better job than business in allying themselves with the world's resentments, then calling those resentments into battle against multinationals. To counterbalance this, Pagan advises:

> Think politically. Overcome a natural aloofness and protectiveness. Become aware of the concerns of others. Reach out for ongoing dialogue with many new publics, whose understanding business needs. The goal, very bluntly, is survival.

Think in advance, Pagan advises, of the consequences of closing a factory, or of not renewing a mining concession or a contract with a farm owners' association. Explain the reasons for actions or nonactions—their immediate and long-term benefits or their costs, and why they might have to be borne by local interests. When necessary, we will have to open our files to show continuity in our policies and responsibility to our consumers and other publics. Most of all, in every action we take we must indicate that we are truly aware of the world around us. Only in that way can we justify our continued existence, the privilege we have to create wealth for ourselves and others.[2] These statements come from a business school classroom and from Nestlé's painful encounters selling their baby formula in Third World countries.

To executives still unbloodied by public crises, Lodge's and Pagan's advice may seem extreme. The initial banality and repetitiveness of danger sometimes lull even the wary. However, the prudent manager considers the powerful, expensive impacts of external events on companies in just the past few years—the oxygen of publicity, as Margaret Thatcher calls it. In the decade to come, communications, internal and external, will be the catalyst of early warnings and solutions—if it is understood, respected, and encouraged to function as it should and can. As will be demonstrated several times, the event in itself may not be as expensive as the public aftermath.

Many trends and external conditions must be factored into running a company and into communications. But too often a wall is erected between what is happening and how the public perceives it; between operating managers faced with harsh realities and staff, who often think business can go on as usual despite everything. At a recent day-long brainstorming at a large multinational, public relations people, despite drastic changes in operating and competitive environments, prattled on with clichés thirty years stale, invoking corporate deities in support of their irrelevant positions. Nostalgics are fun, comfortable, even intelligent, but not functional. Knowing yesterday and just what is comfortable is not enough anymore. Many business failures and detrimental public performances are not simply the fault of limited resources and unscrupulous competition, but of the poverty of imagination that keeps a manager from breaking out of traditional modes; that restricts solutions to the manageable and thinkable.

When trouble hits, shifting tactics daily, personal strength, and resolution will count for far more than all the plans ever written. It is hubris to think public crises can be controlled. The best the battle-scarred executive can hope for is damage control—countering outrageous criticism and telling the truth day after day until it gets across. Never doubt the resourcefulness or tenacity of your adversaries, nor the willingness of the public to believe the worst of the best companies.

For some executives, such tactics will involve crossing from the private,

structured arena of corporate life into high public visibility, either individ-
ually or at the head of their companies.

Such a transition was a culture shock "like suddenly moving to a very foreign country" for W. Michael Blumenthal, former chairman and chief executive officer of Bendix, now of Burroughs, who served as Secretary of the
Treasury under President Carter. In a *Fortune* interview, "Candid Reflections of a Businessman in Washington," he explained the major differences.
An important one was between appearance and reality. At Bendix, the reality—the bottom line—determined whether someone succeeded or failed. In
government, which lacks a bottom line, you can be successful if you appear
to be. And that is largely determined by how you appear to the press. Blumenthal also counseled that you must express yourself very carefully, building
a defense against being misquoted or misunderstood. Some code words you
must avoid; others you can use to state a certain proposition. Eventually,
you learn how to use public statements to shape, influence, and enunciate
policies.[3]

Former Mobil President William P. Tavoulareas crossed from private to
public very differently—with media allegations that he had used Mobil
resources to establish his son in a shipping business, resulting legal actions,
and a book, *Fighting Back*. Although known as a hard-nosed trader, Tavoulareas was shocked by the *Washington Post*'s intransigence, by the impact of
the publicity on his personal life and his son's—and by his legal fees.

Catching trends vital to any business is as elusive as trying to hold quick-
silver in one's palm. In addition to the many techniques discussed elsewhere
in this book, two might be mentioned here: one, looking back to look ahead;
the other, looking at established structures from a different point of view.

In her foreword to *The Distant Mirror*, Barbara Tuchman sees reflections
of the fourteenth century in our own—parallel phenomena to the aftermaths
of the Black Death of 1348–1350 and World War I. She lists economic
chaos, social unrest, high prices, profiteering, depraved morals, lack of production, industrial violence, frenetic gaiety, wild expenditures, luxury,
debauchery, social and religious hysteria, greed, avarice, maladministration,
and the decay of manners. We now have, she concludes, a greater "fellow-
feeling for a distraught age" whose rules were breaking down under the
pressure of adverse and violent events, a kinship with "a period of anguish"
when there is no sense of an assured future.[4]

A different viewpoint also gives new insights. Through his drawings, artist
David Macauley forces us to look up at New York from the tangle of subterranean pipes and tubes, or to study a modern motel as an archeological

site. Journalist Joel Garreau, by dividing North America functionally into nine nations, reveals communications and marketing opportunities obscured by conventional state lines. MexAmerica obliterates the U.S.–Mexican border, which function, migration, and language have already accomplished. Postindustrial America gives insights to the plight—and perhaps the rebirth—of New England. Each of his nations forces a very valuable exercise in analyzing afresh. In that spirit of taking a fresh look, the following trends will be important to companies generally and to their communicators.

• **First:** power and wealth will shift from the European Museum and the eastern United States to the Pacific Rim. The twenty-first century will be dominated not just by Japan but other strong Asian economies and the U.S. West Coast. Communicators will face racially, linguistically, and nationally mixed labor and management, and U.S. citizens will be working for managers and companies from other nations. Press relations will become more complex; overseas media is often government owned and controlled and may be more tendentious than ours.

• **Second:** the new breed of workers will be as driven by their projects as the computer experts in *The Soul of a New Machine.* Or they may be hackers—adventurers, visionaries, risk-takers, and artists—who infuse the marketplace with a new ethic. They will seek unlimited access to information, to anything that can teach them something. Mistrustful of authority, hackers will espouse decentralization. Although tough competitors, they will seek cooperation. Other workers may become disaffected, may drop out, or may lack the common bond of information and skills upon which motivation could be built in the past.

• **Third:** we will suffer an overdose of information. Everyone will have unlimited access to the glut, but few will understand the material or be able to make it work. Ronald Rumsfeld likens this to trying to drink from a large fire hose. Richard B. Madden, chairman and CEO of Potlatch, warns that too much information could produce a fascination with manipulating numbers at the expense of other important goals, such as quality. You can become too remote from the shop floor, he says, if you're sitting behind a large electronic console trying to solve every problem with a new and very expensive by-the-numbers solution.[5] (Or, I might add, if you are operating like a corporate ostrich, with your head hidden in a very comfortable corporate suite.)

• **Fourth:** can any executive doubt after Bhopal, Tylenol, Contac, and the Dalkon Shield that liabilities—legal, public, and product—will increase? Many of the cases in this book demonstrate that the most effective way to mitigate the risk of this trend at its flood is to ask again, and again, and again, what a particular flaw or fault would look like spread widely in public. Operations and executives must be squeaky clean. This advice is not the last gasp of a Puritan ethic, but a sensible means of protection and profitability, even survival. Chester Burger, who has counseled many companies through crises, warns that public opinion will always believe the worst about you unless you tell your side honestly, completely—and very quickly.

• **Fifth**: as business continues in the public spotlight, executives will not be able to hide anything from searching investigations conducted by government agencies, the media, or their own board of directors.

• **Sixth**: as broadcasting and to a lesser extent the print media become show biz, sheer entertainment, business must learn to work within those parameters, however distasteful and mindstretching that is. Corporate performers must learn to compete, cosmetically at least. A television appearance can spell disaster for an executive who does not appear sartorially perfect and in charge, or who wants to convey anything more than a single noncontroversial point.

• **Seventh**: Can so many lemmings be wrong? Whatever the industry trend, too many think, "me too." When the fad was to acquire companies, everyone who could, did. When sell was the cry, it was difficult to avoid that cliché. If everyone else is overcharging on government contracts, we can too. Right? Wrong, as several defense contractors discovered. Procedures and administrators change. The press gets on a hot topic, such as military contracts or white-collar crime, and suddenly the widely acceptable is in the headlines as an example of guilt.

• **Eighth**: problem-solving will be more complex and probably more public. It will be very difficult to duck questions on rampant management turnover, maturing markets, a dearth of new products, and excessive debt created by leveraged buyouts. Nor will public and investor attention be deflected easily by the razzle-dazzle of a new acquisition. That strategy is a bit like Argentina and England going to war over a cluster of remote islands, partly to distract attention from inflation and terrorism at home. It worked, but only briefly. The difficulties resurfaced, compounded by more debt and the war casualties.

• **Ninth**: entrepreneurism should be mentioned, although it is perhaps overdiscussed. Peter Drucker predicts that entrepreneurism may be a major turning point. Already it has put greater sinew and innovation into communications, particularly among employees, and has forced convincing explanations of the boom and bust of some products and bright star performers.

• **Tenth:** current turbulence should be viewed as natural, creative, and eventually productive of stronger organizations. Dr. Rollo May writes that necessary creative chaos must be worked through as old forms crack and new ones either have not emerged or are not recognized for what they are. As painful for many as greenmail, takeovers, executive revolving doors, and rapidly shifting corporate sands are, they can perhaps be viewed as a renewal. The decade of 1973–1983 brought extreme turbulence: the energy crisis, the near collapse of smokestack industries, two sizable recessions, and a gradual understanding that the United States is no longer the preeminent economic power. Can all these factors be positioned as creative chaos, rather than decline?

In addition to these and other general business and social trends of which communicators must be intelligently and eternally aware, four specifically concern communicators: CEOs demanding a great deal more productivity, newsworthy business leaders ducking the press, increasing use of weasel words, and the troubles and obsolescence some traditional communicators are bringing down on themselves.

Few observers have watched public relations as long and as thoughtfully as Harold Burson, chairman of Burson Marsteller. Once, he notes, the principal requisite for public relations was a typewriter, mimeograph machine, mailing lists, and knowledge of newspaper, magazine, and wire service contacts. As others point out, the PR person was looked up on as the official mouthpiece and cheerleader, not the skeptic he should be. Although the practitioner was often a newspaper writer "who sold out for money," he was usually supervised by a salesman, engineer, or administrator.

In the 1960s, Burson explains, public relations became less focused on the press and more oriented toward television; it was forced to cope with a much more complex society. The former stereotypical newspaper man was replaced by a variety of specialists, trained in a broad spectrum of disciplines, who gravitated toward problem-solving. Companies began moving away from blatant advocacy to a more sophisticated total system.

It is now apparent, according to Burson, that economic forces are driving corporate change. Clients are not interested in doing good and getting credit for it—the dominant aim of practitioners of the gray flannel suit generation. Today, the industrial milieu—realistic, pragmatic, cost-effective, and less ideological—has focused concern on nothing less than survival. Executives are not interested in communications, per se, but in what it can do for them. They want results, not systems or platitudes. They don't want to talk about employee communications, but how that contributes to productivity. They don't want to talk about annual reports, but how they affect the value of the stock and the ability to raise funds. Nor to talk about marketing public relations, but about products moving off the shelves or out of dealer showrooms. Nor about government relations except as a means to an end. Contrary to Marshall McLuhan, Burson concludes, the *act* is the message. What we do communicates more clearly than what we say.[6]

Another trend, which seems to fly in the face of all practical considerations, is the refusal of executives to be interviewed, even for favorable articles. Just a few recent examples: Robert Fomon of E.F. Hutton, and John Welch and Donald Grierson of General Electric all declined to be interviewed by *Fortune*. Carl Reichardt, CEO of Wells Fargo Bank, gave the same response, although *The New York Times* piece on Wells' purchase of Crocker Bank was generally favorable. Harry Gray refused *Business Week*. Even that maven of public presence, Ned Gerrity, once senior vice president of ITT, declined. Although these executives undoubtedly had good reasons, they still risked having their company's story told poorly, adversely, or not at all by those far less informed or favorably disposed toward the company.

The third trend important to communicators is the spreading use of weasel, pallid, rubber, or outright deceptive words. Weasel words, which each manager can define as he likes or to his benefit, end up subverting original thoughts or instructions. Thus was demonstrated tragically as instructions from Rockwell and others were filtered up the NASA command structure. Some call this a language of mutilation—turning English into the linguistic equivalent of junk food. Buzz words not only irritate through their overuse (think how many times "bottom line" is used by those who lack any inkling of what a bottom line really is), but they pollute already muddy waters. Whatever happened to speaking plainly?

And finally, as will be discussed in the next section, some communicators—who should be moving ahead of the times, standing terror watch, and doing preventive analysis—are shooting themselves in the foot. The communications officer must be the harbinger of change, demonstrating in a farsighted way how changes and trends will affect his company. He may find himself the designated scapegoat, particularly in media relations, but that risk comes with the turf. Only those battle-tested in corporate warfare or in the more treacherous and dangerous areas of public perceptions can even begin to guide managers safely across the mine fields laid by constituencies, media, advocates for many causes, and sometimes disgruntled employees. If the communicator is looking backward or viewing the future as more of the same, his counsel will be worth little.

## Endangered Communicators: Or, The Lawyers Will Get Them If They Don't Smarten Up

During the public relations boom years in the late 1950s and 1960s, practitioners navigated by unjustifiably rosy crystal balls, foreseeing only further growth and enhanced power. They disdained reporting to anyone but the CEOs, and felt that writing a news release, or even an annual report, was beneath their professional dignity. Press relations was a grubby task to be delegated to a yeoman, a specialist, or a recent convert from journalism. Superstars counseled—whatever that meant.

But several strategic mistakes undermined prestige and profit in the mid-1980s. Instead of studying management, finance, law for the layman, and industry marketing trends, the "professionals" caviled endlessly about how management did not understand or appreciate communicators. Such a we–they stance only predetermined that "they" would win and "we" be consigned to irrelevance. It is self-destructive for anyone reporting to or in senior management not to learn how peers talk, think, and plan; not to immerse himself in the very spirit of the company.

Second, as communication needs and techniques, companies, and competition were changing drastically, so-called professionals prattled on about accreditation, professionalism, and whether New York City dominated the Public Relations Society of America. Annual society meetings became mostly fluff and puff. Job hunters hounded the senior practitioners who showed their faces. Students bounded around assuring everyone that they really liked people—the most often cited and most useless reason for seeking a public relations job.[7] Ignored were the meat and thrust of the job today and in the future. Ignored, too, were executives from other disciplines taking power in communications.

Lawyers, financial types, MBAs, and human resources staff were demonstrating that they knew how to communicate effectively and were winning the hearts and minds of senior management. Communicators had boxed themselves into a defensive position, thus leaving the field open to the apparently more savvy.

The recent spate of booster books, speeches, and articles touting the public relations boom only proves the axiom that when something is shouted about, it's usually no longer important, or is dying.

Communicators must recapture their former respect and demonstrate anew their unique skills and effectiveness. Otherwise, some cussed-minded and farsighted communicators predict a splintering of functions that were formerly centralized: investor relations to finance, employee communications to human resources, press relations to the legal department, and speech writing to one specialist—perhaps a do-all assistant to the CEO. When other skills or extra hands are needed, outside firms will be hired.

These difficulties surfaced dramatically in 1985, which was not a particularly propitious year for communicators. They lost the most ground in corporations, where salaries, prestige, and power are the greatest. Takeovers, mergers, and the downsizing of corporate staffs—actions essential to surviving leaner financial times at home and tougher competition off-shore—meant fewer corporate positions and activities. Killing off the glossy company magazine or dropping image advertising gets the austerity message across very quickly. In many cases, these cutbacks are long gone. Cutting now is much more painful and involves people.

Troubles among formerly high-flying high-tech companies—particularly in California's Silicon Valley—and GE's reduction of its once large and greatly respected news bureau network, meant the loss of many more corporate and counseling jobs. Acquisitions and mergers among public relations firms (for example, Saatchi and Saatchi's purchase of the Rowland Company) and ICPR's bankruptcy further reduced opportunities. And some firms were afflicted by the very woes they counsel against—public troubles.[8]

It seems ironic. At the same time that companies are suffering badly from mangled media relations and bungled public opportunities, the people trained to help the most are either shooting themselves in the foot, or nattering away as if nothing has changed. Courageous communicators are still trying to alert management to possible bad news and public liabilities, sometimes successfully; still trying to demonstrate the sinew and value of communications as an integral part of management and as a way of achieving business goals and controlling damage. Informally, many senior practitioners are meeting over dinner to share wisdom, lick wounds, and get ready intelligently and pragmatically for a tough tomorrow.

# What's in a Name:
# Disagreement and Searching

A name, broad yet precise enough to encompass the myriad ways a corporation communicates, internally and externally, is not only difficult to agree upon. The search itself often fails and confuses rather than illuminates. Some names reflect little more than a current fad, are too restrictive, or connote the worst rather than the best communications can offer management.

One illustration documents the dilemma. The 1984 Hill and Knowlton annual report cover lists thirty-five separate experiences—many of them multiple—in attempting to explain the services a counseling firm offers clients. They range from the mundane and expected—proxy solicitation, shareholder list analysis, and merger and acquisition/takeover communications—to the more exotic satellite services and audio-visual productions, destination marketing, initial public offering, and leveraged buy-out communications.[9]

"Corporate communications," narrow and confused as it can be with telephone systems, computer software, even body language, is used increasingly by major companies. In 1985, 112 of the *Fortune 500* companies called their departments corporate communications—more than any other title or any previous year. It is probably more complete and clearer than other choices. Public relations—once the standard term—is being supplanted because of its narrowness, its less-than-professional connotation among some executives, and its old-fashioned feeling.

Edward Bernays encouraged the use of "public relations counsel" to connote both two-way communications (publicity was one-way) and expert counsel. He attempted to capture some of the authority and prestige of a legal counsel. (Some are still trying today.) Bernays considered PR counsel the giving of professional advice to clients on public relations, regardless of whether or not such advice resulted in publicity.

Not everyone defines public relations so benignly. H.R. Haldeman understood it as the use of techniques to badger, bully, bribe, entice, and persuade people to your side, which could be accomplished only by organizing, orchestrating, and hammering away. William Safire notes that Nixon aides called their brand of news management public relations, but "As a professional p.r. man, Haldeman was merely a good ad man."[10]

"Public affairs," often synonymous with government relations, is not broad enough either and carries with it the faint scent of sensuality. Public information or liaison, popular among nonprofit organizations and government offices, excludes a company's important internal audiences. To some the term seems Orwellian. Marketing, advertising, and investor relations are too specific, unless a department is restricted to those functions. If so, it cannot fully supply all the communications needs important to management. Finally, business is too sophisticated and competitive today to return to the name or the practices of press agents, who began, like Bernays, slipping juicy tidbits favorable to their clients to newspaper columnists.

By default—until a better name emerges—"corporate communications" will be used to describe activities most vital to senior management and directors. These generally include comprehensive strategy, positioning the company with its many constituencies, planning for major crises, and fostering favorable, accurate public perceptions. These broad goals are implemented by a number of activities, such as the communications officer's counsel with peers in senior management, media relations, internal and external publications, financial public relations, speech writing, and monitoring key external individuals and events. To succeed, communications must be embedded in the company's business plans, strategy, and marketing, as well as sensitively aware of the trends and needs of our times.

Three topics—employee communications, advocacy advertising, and government relations—will be discussed only generally. Employee communications is a specialized challenge, increasingly sensitive as workforces, even middle managers, become more mobile and less loyal to a lifetime employer. As workers seek more information from visual rather than traditional print sources, bulletin boards become television monitors and in-house newspaper magapapers become akin to *U.S.A. Today,* which combines many photographs with small amounts of print and snippets of stories. Relationships are shifting among an employee, his manager, and his company. As V.R. Buzzotta pointed out in a recent *New York Times* column ("A Quiet Crisis in the Work Place"), takeovers and mergers are undermining job satisfaction and producing a deep disaffection, most precipitously in managerial ranks. This trend is fostering a quiet frustration "in the collective heart of our work force." He calls for "a rededication to employees on the part of all managers to redress the problem."[11]

Experts working in industries with traditionally strong labor unions see a new relationship emerging. Labor is becoming more multinational, seeks more participation in decision-making, and asks "why" more frequently. And the bitter news of layoffs, health hazards, and the economic need for greater efficiencies are difficult stories, which must be told well and convincingly.

For advocacy or issue advertising—distinct from product advertising—space is purchased in a newspaper to explain a particular company point of view, or to rebut one inimical to the company.[12] Such advertising often rides a chairman's pet hobbyhorse, but also is used widely during tender fights and to explain company positions on strikes, legislation, or what it is doing to counter a disaster. Mobil and United Technologies are perhaps best known for their advocacy advertising. Although effective only if intimately linked with general communications, advocacy advertising is specialized and not needed in every corporation.[13]

Finally, relations between government and corporations, although not as inflamed under the Reagan administration as under previous presidencies, is still a vital interface for any company. However, it is also a specialized function, usually centered on personal lobbying and Washington, D.C.

# 2

# Bottom Line vs. Front Page

## Corporate Relations with the Media

> Journalism is an extraordinary and terrible privilege.
> —Oriana Fallaci

SENIOR executives often come to media relations either bloodied or virginal. Few understand—or even want to—how the media works, the pressure journalists face, and how differing judgments about what is news create adversarial relations. "Sue the bastards," "stonewall them," the ubiquitous but potentially damaging "no comment," and "Why are they hounding me?" are uttered frequently by despairing executives. Others entertain the naive hope that the press can be controlled, ordered about like subordinates. Too few today—on either side—display trust and good intentions. Media complains of lack of access (particularly to the CEO), less-than-complete candor, delayed or no response to queries, talking only in good times, and blatantly building a case for the company.

Yet, there is common ground; the opportunity for understanding does exist. The best trained reporters share with the most progressive corporate leaders the aim to provide the most accurate possible public portrait of the company, its operations, and future prospects. Individuals on both sides are under intense pressure, vulnerable to paying mightily for just one mistake. Both worlds are small. Experiences can be shared intimately and intelligently only with those who have sustained the same defeats and rejoiced over the same successes. Some executives and journalists are high-flying successes, well-known names; others are the unsung, unappreciated grunts doing a good job. Both view the other as all-powerful, aloof, and shielded from the pressures and pains of ordinary mortals. Both are, of course, wrong.

## Media and Business: A Common Ground?

Despite verbal sniping across the barricades, media and business share many concerns and interests. Senior business executives and well-known journalists explored these at a 1977 meeting in Princeton, N.J. Participants Joseph A. Califano, Jr., and Howard Simons noted that the antagonism boils down to "business builds up; media tears down."[1] "Business always hides its wrongdoing, only the media penetrates" the stone wall. Business, concerned with its public image, is eager to put its best foot forward; the press wants a good story. Executives may complain about shallow, superficial, biased coverage, but that doesn't mean they really want comprehensive, thoughtful, fair coverage. Every large organization or person has potentially embarrassing secrets.

Media criticizes business for stonewalling, unavailability, giving just the agreed-upon company line but no more, and elusive executives, who seem to live private, privileged, sheltered lives. (The perceived difference in earnings, perks, power, and lifestyles is an unspoken irritant.)

Complaints come from both sides: some bred of half-knowledge; others better founded. Business leaders call the media too powerful and sensational; they accuse it of writing about the bad news, never the good; and they charge that reporters oversimplify or just don't understand what they are writing about.

Executives at the conference wished aloud that reporters knew the difference between a stock and a bond, net and gross; and that those covering economic matters had taken a course in economics—and passed it. Many reporters cared or knew little about the company they were covering. Until the 1970s foreign affairs and politics, even sports, were the sought-after reporting jobs. Unattractive, below even show biz, was business reporting. Some business reporters on local newspapers also sold advertising space. But in the past decade, the big stories have been business and economics: inflation, unemployment, investment incentives, major bankruptcies, deficits, giant takeovers, and prospects for the free market.

As economics and business became a prestige beat, reporters demonstrated much better, wider knowledge. Many hold MBAs. Although general economic coverage has increased vastly in quality and quantity, individual companies or industries are largely overlooked. The old tradition that any mention of a company is free publicity still lurks in many a media mind. Only an event too momentous to ignore—a fire, strike, giant layoffs, a Bhopal-type disaster—is covered, fueling the criticism that the press emphasizes the negative.

As Louis Banks, a former *Fortune* managing editor, asked the press, why do they hate you out there? Banks cited careless news stories, chronic negativism, and "ignorant reporting that tangles business complexities into erroneous conclusions or ducks complexities in favor of power struggles and personality clashes, real or imagined."[2] In the urge to simplify, the press may fasten on a single, obvious, but not necessarily important quality of a public figure: the Iron Magnolia for Rosalynn Carter or arrogance for Alexander Haig. Television with its relentless time constraints suffers from this problem even more acutely. Criticism, once directed solely against newspapers, has been deflected by television. Its equipment is intrusive and potentially dangerous in a factory setting. Even a complex story must be restricted to thirty to ninety seconds on the air. A good, fair, talented journalist finds it difficult to probe a controversial, complex subject within such constraints.

Many difficulties are systemic to all journalism: deadlines, limited news space, competition with other media, and personal quirks—the different metabolisms, skills, sources, and perceptions of individual editors and reporters.

Lewis H. Young, for many years the editor of *Business Week*, points out that the business view is often out of focus because it understands neither the reporter's job nor how to play up to media needs.

Misperceptions spring not from inaccuracy, but from a difference in viewpoint between reporter and company. "As outsiders, journalists are . . . immune to the internal vested interests—the politics, the history of a decision, especially the prejudices, biases and pressures on decision-makers."[3] This encourages some business people to still believe that journalists are biased against business, ignorant of industry, sensation-seeking, and fundamentally unfair.

Another area of conflict is news judgment. Young gives his criteria for a good business story: a company does exceptionally well or poorly; conflicts surface between companies, business, and government, or among executives; a breakthrough development or striking new idea is announced. But rather than understand what motivates the media, its strengths and weaknesses, many executives carp or turn cynical, bite their tongues or try to foist company-serving stories as news. Other businessmen, such as Felix Rohatyn, the Lazard Freres partner who chairs New York City's Municipal Assistance Corporation, and Irving Shapiro, former DuPont CEO, learn to work with the media as successful politicians do. This skill requires developing a thick skin to withstand criticism and a willingness to learn from each encounter. The rewards? Young lists better investor relations, increased sales, higher employee morale, and fewer labor problems.

Neither side seems to accept that what is good for the goose is good for the gander. One issue—disclosure of interests—illustrates this. Business is both private and public. Financial interests, board appointments, individual or corporate positions in other companies, family ties and holdings must be made public. But reporters have cried foul—often and loudly—at any attempt to determine whether they hold stock in a company they are covering or whether a family member stands to gain financially. Professional and personal lives should be kept separate, except when they influence news. When a reporter and a source are linked romantically, and each is an avaricious careerist; when information traded in pillow talk shows up in newspaper headlines, usually leaked and unavailable to competition or to the subject of the story, then that relationship is fair game for questions and revelation. And in the case of R. Foster Winans, convicted of profiting from information gained by writing the *Wall Street Journal's* "Heard on the Street" column, his roommate was a factor, and was so reported by the *Journal.*[4]

When John C. Behrens began contacting well-known reporters for interviews, he found paranoia common. Some never answered his calls at all, and others only after repeated calls. One shunted Behrens to his lawyer. Most questioned him closely about the reasons for his interest. Although eager to ask others about income, journalists don't entertain questions about their own and its sources from speaking, newsletters, and syndicated columns.[5]

Such double standards cloud the issues of confidentiality and competition. Revealing sources of information is an issue a journalist would risk jail to protect—and some have. But the press leaps eagerly on business or government secrets. During the Princeton meetings, a television executive said that he would not wait a day or two to go with a story about a CIA agent, even though it might cost the agent his life; a competitor might scoop him. How would the press react if a pharmaceutical company rushed a product to market to beat its competition?

Until recently, businesses operated under considerably less scrutiny than today. They were often shadowy powers in their communities and foreign countries. Often CEOs played *éminence grise.* Some newspapers were company-owned: Anaconda owned papers in Montana; DuPont only recently sold its Wilmington, Delaware, newspapers; United Fruit published several newspapers in Central America. Even large newspapers once ran company handouts. It was great sport among the public relations people, often put down as hacks by reporters, to compare releases issued by a major counseling firm against "news coverage" in the next day's business pages.[6] President Lyndon Johnson, no fan of the press, was convinced that reporters were merely transmission belts for shrewd public relations people.[7] But journalistic Prufrocks, measuring their lives in handouts, are discredited by the best of their peers.

Despite important differences, both sides share interests. Business, as it operates increasingly on the consent of its various publics, must assume the risks of heightened exposure and accessibility. It must argue its position vigorously and confidently, not shrinking from controversy. Conversely, reporters and editors need to educate themselves about economics, international competition, the mechanics of doing business, large organizational structures, and ways of decision-making. A truly fine newspaper cannot be a public relations operation, a business blotter, or a booster for the community, but it should be accurate and fair.

## Watergate: A Sea Change

Journalism is slow moving and tradition-bound. It refuses to budge until it is shoved by some irresistible external force. The shove came: competition from electronic media, change in reporting techniques, dying newspapers, plus a burst of new technology, which explosively speeded up the transmission and processing of information.

The once-vaunted objectivity in reporting began to be criticized as a guise for superficiality, even mindless neutrality. Some reporters began to feel caged by old formulas—each story had to have a neat point and start with hard news, even if based on some phony staged event. It had to impose some meaning, however superficial or spurious, on often insignificant, mysterious, or downright absurd happenings.

A bias developed toward negative news, toward conflict and controversy. This bias often distorted coverage far more extensively than the frequently discussed ideological slants, such as automatically being antibusiness. Some reporters, swept away by the passions of the moment, rushed past or ignored important, more complicated issues and ideas.

Georgie Anne Geyer, formerly a respected foreign correspondent, now a columnist, has explained the changes that were induced by Watergate. In the late 1950s, as a reporter for Chicago's feisty *Daily News,* she covered fires, murders, or investigations. "We did not write columns or inject our personal interpretations on the news page," she noted. It was a "much straighter," much more "honest job" than now. Staff reporters competed brutally with other papers, but not with each other, unlike the *Washington Post*, where everyone was pitted against everyone else. They worked for prizes, not for the readers.

According to Geyer, we were reporters, not journalists—and certainly not media celebrities. "Nobody came into journalism for power." Some came because they wanted to write. Others were attracted by a view of life or by the excitement not afforded elsewhere. The new breed of journalists became "arbiters of truth," moralists who mistook relative judgment for absolute moralism. They began to "judge and criticize, to take it upon themselves to reform, if not the world" at least their own evil country. They saw "goodness everywhere but at home." They began a love affair with advocacy, which hit government first, but did not leave the private sector unscathed.[8]

Watergate coverage glorified the gumshoe drudgery of leg-work, fact-gathering. Many reporters succumbed to an almost detective-like cloak-and-dagger fever, ready to probe the murky depths of clandestine corruption. Some young journalists, especially from television, tended to skip over telling the reader just the facts—a straight recitation of what happened—to concentrate on the more exciting speculation about backstage maneuverings, personalities, and often specious predictions. In their defense, frequently the backstage and publicly obscured is ultimately more important. Henry Kissinger's publicly announced illness in India covered his precedent-breaking covert trip to China. Likewise, bland announcements of corporate departures obscure protracted struggles and personality clashes.

If Watergate produced important changes, Vietnam brought others. To Geyer, writers covering the war assumed the right and duty to make the most astonishing judgments to change society through their writings—not merely to report or reflect, but to redeem it. She views this shift as dangerous, nearly destroying truth in journalism. Other writers became heavily influenced by movements: environmentalism, consumerism, feminism, Naderism, and the new left. Many of the journalists routinely assumed that these groups were right—hence government and business were wrong.

Actually, the changes were a mixed bag. In his study and interviews of "typewriter guerrillas," John C. Behrens, a professor of journalism, outlines qualities typical of the best of the post-Watergate reporters. They cajole, compromise, berate, badger, and hassle people; can be insufferable asses, unintelligible mystics, and tough adversaries.

But, Behrens warns, the tough exterior is vulnerable. Although outwardly abrasive, strident, and moralistic, the best must also have unusual sensibilities and intelligence, curiosity, and a high degree of skepticism. They must be able to bluff their way to information. Tenacity and perseverance are needed to get information from someone who does not want the reporter to have it. Long-term investigations, distinct from straight reporting, are very lonely work, devoid of the camaraderie and instant gratification of seeing a story appear immediately that sustain other reporters. Some reporters approach a story with swift, almost hurricane force. Others use the telephone as deftly as an expert surgeon wields his scalpel. Still others, such as I.F. Stone, discover important stories by laboriously reading every document issued on a given subject.

Only when a business spokesperson understands where the journalist is coming from, the pressures and competition he faces, can the communicator stand a good chance of getting his company's message across effectively. Or, possibly, at all.

One *Fortune 100* CEO, hounded, bewildered, raked over by some of the toughest investigative writers, and deeply troubled by what intense national media visibility was doing to his company and its management, exploded: "Why are they doing this to us?" To supplement the painful insights he was receiving on the public battlefield and from his own staff, his communications officer gave him three cautionary tales in press relations.

First he read Heinrich Böll's *The Lost Honor of Katharina Blum*, a chilling account of a young German woman falsely accused and defamed by the sensationalist press. "The reporters were relentless," the CEO reacted. Precisely the point! Granted, Böll's account is highly dramatized; however, it illustrates the possible harassment not only of a target, but of every associate and family member. In the story, the police, while leaking information to the press, delve into intimate details. Alarming changes in Katharina's behavior take place. She becomes almost totally apathetic—bombarded by epitaphs from neighbors, pornographic mail, and unpleasant propositions. Few seemed to question the newspaper slanders, lies, and distortions. But they altered the lives of the otherwise rational people around Katharina—like her employer, who wanted to rig up a Molotov cocktail to toss through the newspaper's windows. Eventually, after avoiding them, she agreed to meet the photographer and reporter for an exclusive interview. She killed them. When the film version was shown in New York City, one audience clapped. As Louis Banks has warned the press: they hate you out there.

Individuals who have never been the target of such media harassment may deem Böll's tale overdrawn. But is it? Mary Cunningham, in *Powerplay*, describes her feelings of being hunted and betrayed while she was in the eye of a media blitz. Every telephone call zings; every public appearance is a cat-and-mouse game. Tragically, deaths *can* result from sensational, distorted coverage. The essentially private business executive, unlike public figures more inured and accustomed to visibility and criticism, withers and worries with exposure. Even seeing words quoted accurately in headlines or broadcast for millions can sting and disconcert. They are so public.

The second book the CEO tackled, Carl Bernstein's and Robert Woodward's *All the President's Men*, details step-by-step how the authors sleuthed information on Watergate. One of their tactics, important to corporate media relations, was to approach lower-level employees—particularly executive secretaries—who may have important information and be willing to talk. Bernstein tells of knocking on the front door of a small tract house in suburban Washington. He thought the resident, a bookkeeper, might know a great deal. She worked for Maurice Stans. Many so approached were not willing to talk, but enough did to give the *Washington Post* reporters their story. Watergate itself, the two reporters' techniques, plus their subsequent stardom produced a sea change in how news is gathered and reported.

The CEO's third cautionary tale came from *Boys on the Bus*, Timothy Crouse's account of reporters covering George McGovern's presidential campaign. The book illustrates the competitive, bone-wearying pressure cooker in which reporters work. Often the surface and the reality are contradictory. A giddy camaraderie mixes with fear and low-grade hysteria. The dangers are great. If reporters file a story late or make a glaring factual error, they risk losing everything. "When it came to writing," Crouse observes, "they were as cautious as a diamond cutter."

The bus's womb-like ambience, the closed circles of high-powered journalism, produced what Crouse calls a "notorious phenomenon—pack (herd or fuselage) journalism." Trapped on the same bus or plane, reporters ate, drank, gambled, and compared notes with the same colleagues week after week. Off the bus, socially, they saw the same people, used the same sources, belonged to the same background groups, swore by the same omens. "They arrived at their answers just as independently as a class of honest seventh graders using the same geometry text—they did not have to cheat off each other to come up with the same answers." Of course, the same charges of exclusivity and insularity are often brought against corporate management.

Neither a participant nor a bystander, an insider-outsider, the journalist always sees in more depth and earlier than the average person. But some of the most insightful information never reaches the news columns. It is shared among reporters over drinks or, according to Crouse, sent as memos to senior editors as grist for their cocktail circuit.[9]

Another consideration Crouse and others have commented upon is the tendency to blame the reporter an executive sees rather than the invisible editor whose power and role he may not fully understand. But the editor rides in the reporter's psyche on any assignment. Journalists self-censor in anticipation of some imaginary showdown, second-guessing a cautious editor or knowing that they will have to justify a lead different from a competitor's or the wire services. Although reporters may appear rash, bold, or frivolous to a corporate type, they must often play it safe, following the pack, current fads, and cant. This diminishes the fight for scoops, the drive for exclusive information, fresh approaches, or leads.

As a reporter matures, he often develops doubts about his work, questions how he is using his power, and questions how to bridge the difference between the reality he witnesses and what he reports. Reporting, perhaps even editing, is a young person's job. Not just because of the physical pressures—relentless deadlines, irregular hours, constant travel, and junk food—but because of having to jump from one subject to another, never really having time to be immersed in any. With the rise of investigative writing, following Watergate and the extension of the beat system from geography and turf to subject, this was mitigated.[10]

Some individuals view the press as an aggressive monolith. But reporters, even on the same newspaper, compete fiercely among themselves. So does television with print. When television people first appeared on the McGovern press bus, older newspaper reporters regarded them with outright loathing, considered them dilettantes, glamour boys, and know-nothings. Exacerbating these feelings was the dramatic boom in television while newspapers were dying. The breach has been healed somewhat today, but critics still cavil about highly-paid "rip-and-read heads." (Translation: attractive men and women who rip-off stories written by someone else and read them on camera.)

Without question, television has changed news gathering and the way reporters interact with their subjects.[11] Vermont Royster, who for almost fifty years wrote for the *Wall Street Journal*, details how the presidential press conference evolved from the relatively intimate format of FDR's chats with a few reporters in the Oval Office into today's instant visual drama. Some 200 reporters, cameramen, and technicians jam into a conference room and become the stars of the action. Sheer numbers and visibility have replaced free-wheeling conversation with confrontation.

Instant transmission has robbed the president—or anyone on live television—of the chance to "think out loud," perhaps rephrase or hone his questions. "He must live in constant fear of a slip of the tongue; awkward, damaging phraseology beyond recall or correction."[12] So a president hesitates to be frank and open. Reporters cannot share his thought processes, which would help them better inform the public. Nor is there an even moderately satisfactory means of redress, such as a letter to the editor.

Press relations between the U.S. President and the media are vastly different from what corporate leaders experience. No CEO enjoys television networks or reporters eagerly awaiting any word; however, some parallels and lessons apply to both. For all their power, no president ever had prolonged success at muzzling the press. Even President Richard M. Nixon, who perhaps had the most antagonistic relations, eventually learned one crucial lesson: give them lots of news doled out at just the right amount at the right time. The alternative is damaging coverage or reliance on ill-informed, possibly even hostile sources.

# What Does the Media Want?

When business bothers to ask this question the press is quick with suggestions. Carol Loomis, a member of *Fortune*'s board of editors, makes six:

- Staff media relations with bright, pleasant people.

- Make sure they return phone calls from the press promptly, without fail. Saying "no" isn't the ultimate sin; not responding within a reasonable time is.

- Get to know the editors and writers most likely to be involved in a company story. "People on my side of the fence are as susceptible to flattery as everyone else." (Some fault the press for being pushovers for access to powerful and articulate officials.)

- Be helpful on stories, even general industry or trend articles.

- Encourage senior management to be candid and honest with all its audiences, particularly the press. This may seem naive, a bit Boy Scoutish, but once caught in a cover-up or an outright lie, the damage is always worse.

- Open meetings with security analysts to the business press.[13] Although this sounds simple, analysts often resent the intrusion of the press, thinking it would restrain comments or focus them more generally than financially. Journalists and analysts compete for exclusive information. Some companies compromise and hold a special press briefing or interview session immediately following the analyst meeting.

Other business editors suggest better contact, particularly access to CEOs, and understanding of deadlines. Some corporate people try to be cute by calling in a major story at 6 P.M. when they think deadlines will preclude thorough research. Others bother editors with junk, failing to understand there must be a good reason for a story: a news peg. At times the fault is silence—not telling editors about unusual stories or mistakes, or being reluctant to release financial information on subsidiaries or percent of market share. This information, business people point out, might be useful to competitors or raiders looking to pick off a highly profitable division. Both are valid reasons. However, one company refused to give the age and sex of its top six officers, even though such information is routinely available in most annual reports and all 10-Ks.

Adroit and open corporate communication often can turn coverage to a company's advantage. When Hoffman-LaRoche in northern New Jersey announced substantial layoffs, they were cooperative and forthcoming with local reporters. They let reporters talk with employees and participate in out-placement and other meetings. This positioned the layoffs in a positive light and may have deflected probing stories of long-term problems.[14]

Walter Guzzardi, Jr., a member of *Fortune*'s board of editors, has other words of advice on the politics of the press. There is no place to hide, he counsels. If the press is going after you for a story and you duck, many outside sources—disgruntled former employees, hostile competitors, and others—not all favorably inclined toward the company or up-to-date may give the story an undesirable cast.

Guzzardi views the business–press relationship as wary, not adversarial. Mutual needs surmount different perspectives, objectives, and interests. To Guzzardi, distrust exists largely because of deficiencies on both sides. Many people in the press are enormously self-important; they think life should be organized to suit them professionally, even personally. They enjoy the enormous power they wield. Also, the dramatic organization of a story requires extremely pointed ways of making arguments, which inevitably shadow the truth. On the other hand, corporate executives expect too much: that copy appear as they have written it. That's unrealistic. They, too, have an ego screen. "The process of becoming a CEO," comments Guzzardi, "is an enormous ego-feeding experience."[15]

## Mike Fright: The Warfare of Interviewing

Leave a note on any corporate executive's desk reading, "Mike Wallace called about a *60 Minutes* interview," and pangs of genuine anxiety will ensue. Although Wallace may have mellowed recently and the program attacks business less, he was the *bête noire* of executives for many years.

"Mike fright" demonstrates many of the techniques used in interviewing—some would say entrapment—and the evolution of television journalism. Wallace explains the aims of *60 Minutes* and its forerunner, *Night Beat*, in his *Close Encounters, Mike Wallace's Own Story*, written with Gary Paul Gates. Modestly, Wallace explains that the programs became enduring models of thorough preparation and of insistent probing to get at the face behind the mask, the elusive truth behind the nervous evasion. The aim: to stimulate, not avoid, controversy. Guests were thoroughly and painstakingly researched. The formula and staging—often klieg lights glaring over the interviewer's shoulder in the guest's eyes—forced interviewees to come clean and blocked their retreat into amiable reassurance. *Night Beat* used searching, tight close-ups to record tentative glances, nervous tics, and beads of perspiration. Wallace developed techniques not needed in print—brusque interruptions, exaggerated facial gestures, the cigarette as a weapon—as part of his performance.

Anyone who did not prepare himself in background or techniques, who expected an easy, cordial, almost insouciant mood, a light workout, was in for trouble. One guest who worked the *60 Minutes* system well, according to Wallace, was H.R. Haldeman. He was unfailingly courteous, displayed a highly selective memory, and deftly parried attempts to pin him down on Watergate. He answered vaguely and tentatively, yet conveyed the impression of a man trying to be cooperative and forthcoming. Even his evasions seemed credible. He took a difficult or provocative question and smothered it in a morass of detail or hair-splitting qualifications, resulting in confusion or tedium. Haldeman understood that a dull, imprecise interview suited *his* purpose and sabotaged Wallace's. He projected, according to Wallace's assessment, a manner and tone of sincerity that made him credible. By contrast his colleague, John D. Ehrlichmann, sweated and came across as angry and uptight.

Wallace sees television journalism as descended from the muckrakers of the turn of the century. He admits that sometimes *60 Minutes* got carried away in the excitement of the quest, and wound up with stories that conveyed more heat than light, more theater than substance. Television tends to raise disposable issues; topics come and go, fresh diversions change with the seasons and the ratings. To others television thrives on the popular culture, the new—like traditional retailing or theme restaurants.

Two *60 Minutes* interviews of particular business interest involved San Diego Federal and Coors. Dick Carlson, senior vice president of Federal, said he would only participate if his own video crew taped the interview. (One of the most persistent and telling criticisms against the program is highly tendentious film editing and splicing.) Wallace agreed, never imagining that he would be hoist on his own petard. During a halt, while the *60 Minutes* tape was being changed, Federal cameras kept rolling, and caught Wallace's ethnic expletive. When he learned of it, he asked to have the tape erased, but later backed off. Carlson was amused that the master of ambush was caught off guard by his small California savings and loan company.

Joe and Bill Coors decided that they had two choices when the *60 Minutes* staff approached them: tell them to go away, or accept the challenge and open the entire brewery. During the research and interviewing, the crew found that Coors was a victim of a systematic campaign by labor to discredit the company—and they reported it.

Ironically, the unpleasant encounters and fights that Wallace and his crews aroused, the potential damage to some companies and their images, forced business leaders to train for television appearances, to learn how to work the medium. This has spawned a thriving charm school business: firms now teach executives how to talk and parry tough questions, how to dress, and how to appear effectively on television.

Interviewing techniques for questioner and subject are at the heart of such training. Wallace, Georgie Anne Geyer, and Oriana Fallaci—all with differing styles—explain their approaches to interviewing. The most adroit, successful interviewer—but also the most dangerous to the neophyte—is the openly friendly and empathetic reporter. Caught off guard or lulled, the subject may make damaging, emotional, or embarrassing statements. Who can forget Henry Kissinger talking about the Lone Ranger diplomacy to Fallaci? Geyer explains the woman interviewer's advantage. She believes in empathetic immersion, basically a psychoanalytic term meaning immersing yourself: listening intently, sympathizing with interviewee's perceptions, then extracting truths from what was heard or said. Women seem to put men at ease, Geyer writes. "Sooner or later everything pours out. Men forget they are with a journalist" and so respond as they always have to women as listeners and comforters.[16] (Men often will talk in front of women colleagues with the same openness, as if they were invisible and surely no competition or threat.)

Geyer's style contrasts greatly with the more confrontational Oriana Fallaci, the Italian journalist. She considers herself not a cold recorder of what she sees and hears, but a participant, intently observing as though the matter concerned her personally and required her to take a stand. She approaches her subject not with detachment, but armed with provocative questions. Despite all of her preparation, she fears being "a worm hidden in the wood of history"—not having enough eyes, ears, and brains to understand. With the powerful who have been her subjects, she had to exert herself to keep them talking. "It became a game to reach the truth." She sought to draw out the moral drama, the truths never before revealed in public. Some of the comments she elicited made news in themselves.[17]

Wallace uses confrontational tactics also, provoking subjects and attempting to trap the innocent with his friendly manner—between you and me (and millions of viewers). The subject confesses and, zap, Wallace is on him. Even pallid answers to his provocative questions reveal a good deal about the interviewee's character and personality. Wallace considers an interviewee's appearance on television license to probe beneath the carefully constructed layers of public image.

In interviewing, in all media relations, lack of immediate rapport and veracity must be analyzed. The reporter must ask himself, Why are you telling me this? Are you attempting to cover a problem? Hype stock? Promote a career? Speaking for someone hiding from the press for a variety of reasons? Reporters know, for example, that short sellers on Wall Street cultivate the press—probably more successfully than most investors. Highly competitive reporters seek the kind of hard-hitting, insider information the shorts appear to be peddling. Leaking is part of sourcing. Journalism's mythology requires knowing powerful people who leak information for their own or a superior's advantage. Reporters must examine the dynamics of the leak and be judicious using a tip; if a reporter becomes known as a conduit, he jeopardizes his position with other sources and his publication.

## Battling Poor Perceptions:
### Navistar and Iacocca

Businessmen are most reluctant to protest poor reporting, even though many in the media say they welcome reasoned, honest responses. Some executives fear future problems or second- and third-day articles that only drag out the event or bring it to the attention of even more people. But when a situation is protracted and seriously damaging or unfair to a company, business leaders feel increasingly forced to take the offensive.

Donald D. Lennox, chairman and CEO of the International Harvester Company (now Navistar), has talked publicly of reckless reporting that worsened his company's ordeal and then unfairly ignored its turnaround. In 1979 Harvester apparently was having a banner year: a record $369 million in profits on revenues of $8.4 billion. The future looked bright—at least to the outside. Despite the fact that Harvester was a high-cost producer and other sour signals, management continued to be optimistic—too optimistic as it turned out, according to Lennox. Measured against the reality of Harvester's performance, Lennox explained, this optimism was creating credibility gaps with customers, lenders, vendors, and the media, which "recorded the unfolding drama in meticulous, if not always accurate detail." Negative speculation was increased. Caught in a perception bind, Harvester had to make corrective actions abundantly apparent.

First, the CEO Archie McCardell resigned. Drastic measures were taken: severe cutbacks in plant production, sales of assets not deemed critical to ongoing business, furloughs, and layoffs. In the spring of 1982, the media saw news in this saga of a deteriorating giant. "Unfortunately, their research was weak," comments Lennox. "They went beyond reporting facts," injecting their own reactions. Competitors used the quotes to sell against Harvester. Vendors began to question open account terms.

Harvester's management felt that the media had pushed them virtually to the wall, only to ignore their nascent turnaround. "Financially troubled," "ailing," or "failing" seemed inseparable adjectives to Harvester's name. "They left us high and dry, our reputation in tatters and our credibility all but lost." Many publics important to Harvester were being hammered by adverse publicity. Harvester decided its only option was to counterattack. First, they committed scarce dollars and management time to the first corporate advertising campaign in Harvester's history, "On Track . . . And Moving Ahead," supported by supplier newsletters, employee communications, and word of mouth. Executives visited lending institutions, company locations, and major vendors. Lennox concluded that although the price was high in terms of time, dollars, employee morale, and customer confidence, Harvester finally could tell market and customers, "The commitment is forever."

What did Harvester learn? Lennox cites mistakes in what was said and how. "For too long our public forecasts were overly optimistic; we should have been more realistic. We were not as candid, forthcoming nor as accessible to the press as was in the company's interest." However, Lennox also notes the almost cavalier treatment dished out by large segments of the press, which primarily seemed obsessed by writing the company's obituary. "When the patient did not die, we became a nonevent, left by the media publicly bruised and battered."

Lennox concludes, "When the media reports speculation of coming events as facts, when they imply inside sources when it is pure speculation, I believe they have assumed an irresponsible position. Corporate management must be factual, honest, and forthright, make certain they keep the media informed. . . . I believe the media assumes the same responsibilities, when they enter into the dialogue."[18]

In January 1986, Harvester changed its name to Navistar: the final proud recovery. The new name, necessitated by a divestiture of the farm equipment business to Tenneco, Inc., was heralded by an advertising blitz. Ads spoke of crises past: "we weathered one of the most difficult series of crises any American corporation has ever faced." They complimented employees as magnificent, responding to every adversity with hard work, determination, savvy, and guts. After citing financial accomplishments, Navistar pointed out that all the experts had predicted imminent doom. Bankruptcy had been a specter.

Although Lee Iacocca has gained phenomenal positive attention for both his management successes and his autobiography, his assessment of media coverage of Chrysler's financial troubles is much like that of International Harvester's CEO. First, the press jumped the gun by leaking the announcement of his switch to Chrysler from Ford before he had accepted the new position. Then, press coverage of the bailout offered much silly advice. Tom Wicker of *The New York Times* suggested that Chrysler devote its energies to building mass transit equipment instead of automobiles. Editorial cartoonists had a marvelous time. The *Wall Street Journal* called the loans "Laetrile for Chrysler" in one headline. The paper pressed editorially, suggesting that Chrysler "be put out of its misery," "let them die with dignity." Angered by what he considered abusive freedom of the press, Iacocca in a letter to the editor accused the *Journal* of running every single item of bad news, but none of the more hopeful.

After loan guarantees were granted, Iaccoca said the *Wall Street Journal* was still unconvinced. "Although we had enough money," were a restructured company, with a new management, the right product, and quality, the *Journal* kept pointing out that the economy could get worse, as could car sales: "Chrysler, having cut muscle as well as fat, is still in a weak state."

Given such coverage, Iacocca argued that it was not surprising the public had trouble understanding what was going on. Even the terms were confusing: "bail out," although better than handout, implies an inadequate crew that needed help. "We were portrayed as a big monolithic company that did not deserve help." Actually, Iacocca countered, Chrysler was an "amalgam of little groups—suppliers, dealers, and small businessmen, not fat cats, that needed a helping hand, not a hand out. Many people thought we were asking for gifts, or had received $1 billion in cash in a brown paper bag and never had to repay it."

To control public damage and explain Chrysler's new resolves, Iacocca reluctantly became spokesman for the corporate advertising campaign. He feared—unnecessarily as it turned out—that the eternal pitchman wears out his welcome in a disposable society, fickle about its heroes. The advertising visibility and the respect he gained for successfully turning around a large company beset by difficulties in a very competitive market and a soft economy prompted another theme in the *Wall Street Journal:* his hankering for public office.[19]

## Creating Images: Following Fads

Media relations often are used and sometimes abused in creating images of companies, countries, and their leaders. Persona created for presidents and other political leaders are much more visible and much better documented than the quiet work of corporate communications people. However, there are principles and techniques in common.

In *The Splendid Deception,* Hugh Gregory Gallagher explains how the press, secret service, staff, and family cooperated in presenting Franklin D. Roosevelt as vigorous and physically fit—a carefully constructed and artfully maintained image. Throughout his presidency, photographs of FDR being carried, crawling, or fallen were banned. Someone, usually a family member, always bore his weight or helped him rise and locked his heavy leg braces, which were blackened so they would not be obvious.

Just before his death, the president's few public appearances were carefully arranged, widely publicized, and heavily photographed. His skillful press secretary, Steven Early, made full use of releases, statements, short press conferences, and radio talks. Roosevelt continued to dominate the war news, but far from the public eye and the press, who saw only what he wished them to. More recently, it was a well-hidden fact that President Jimmy

Carter—in contrast to the poor peasant farmer image he projected—was a millionaire, personally worth $5 million as an agrobusiness corporate executive.[20]

In business, the best known and most controversial image creator and fad follower is John DeLorean. He spun such a convincing legend that even as his automobile company unraveled, most reporters were still reluctant to look at him closely and critically. Only his arrest on cocaine charges sparked critical attention. (He was ultimately acquitted.) Until then, DeLorean had crafted well.

Early in his career, he spoke to 1960s sensibilities—espousing corporate social responsibility, minority employment, and the "ethical" car. Customers would not only get a car, such as the GTO or later a DeLorean model, but also a part of his personal Horatio Alger dream. The automotive executive excelled in selling the American Dream back to the country. Meanwhile, he molded himself to the current fashion in appearance and personal life. In looks, he played the classic corporate nonconformist. In a day of Brooks Brothers uniforms in corporate suites, he tended to wear turtleneck sweaters, bell-bottom jeans, and a peace symbol on a chain around his neck. However, he disclaimed the maverick role. Professionally, DeLorean left the less-newsworthy field of engineering—many attest that he was an extremely talented executive, a highly skilled engineer and marketing manager—for the more fertile and faddish fields of finance and public relations.

He became a feast for the news-hungry press. The *Detroit Press* found him unusually accessible and always good copy. He came across as brash, egotistic, energetic, and optimistic. His departure from General Motors was portrayed as high moral principle: A gutsy career change and a conquest of mid-life crises, immortalized by Gail Sheehy in *Passages*. He could discuss the Beach Boys, quote Montaigne, or mention ruminations on human misery by social historian Peter Gay. DeLorean listened intently and turned encounters with reporters into casual conversation. The press was caught up with his idea of producing an ethical car. Reporters did not check easily verifiable facts—such as patents granted—or to look for the substance behind the bold rhetoric. Investors and reporters alike were sucked in. Much about DeLorean could blind the most cynical eye.

The maverick auto engineer was too compelling to be deflated by tough journalism. His impressive stack of press clippings was a potent weapon. No other entrepreneur in business history used publicity as well in amassing his seed capital. Nevertheless, the pristine facade began to crumble. Court documents in lawsuits against his company—and later against him personally—

filed across the nation told the other story. They ran beside laudatory media accounts "like photographic negatives."

Foolishly, DeLorean came to believe his press, became a prisoner of his own outsized vision. Like the Wizard of Oz, he scrambled behind a curtain to maintain his credibility, with little concern about the methods he used to keep his reputation and investment intact. But the glamour he cultivated made him prime meat for the media. Periodicals that were previously circumspect about his car company began recycling negative stories. Industry executives who once had only kind words or silence about DeLorean were producing unflattering anecdotes. Even the careful cosmetic presence was falling away: getting aboard a transport bus in a blue prison jump suit, manacles on his hands and legs, did little for his image.[21] As John Hill counseled wisely many years ago, public relations is not a cosmetic, it cannot put a pretty face on a bad situation or an untruth.

Even today, broke, divorced, and under indictment, DeLorean still is cleverly promoting his image. Interviewed in San Francisco, where he was promoting his book, a reporter described him as craggy, the image of a macho national treasure. In maintaining his innocence, he comes across as a modern-day Job, who must endure, persevere, and survive—a scrapper, down but not out.[22]

## Journalists Criticize Themselves

One reason the media fell for the DeLorean fad was their lack of self-criticism. But members of the press do call peers on the carpet, as Tom Goldstein did in *The News at Any Cost: How Journalists Compromise Their Ethics to Shape the News.* He points out that reporters can chase a citizen down the street with cameras rolling and paint a false picture that no subsequent explanation can eradicate. Reporters can entrap the unwary, ambush the unsuspecting, and assume false identification (concealing that they are reporters to gain employment in a plant, for example) to gather information. Some reporters say they resort to the ambush interview when requests for a formal interview are either turned down or are expected to be. Surprise, however, yields dramatic footage, catches the subject saying something he might not have, or might have stated in a less damaging, less headline-grabbing way. The camera allows no qualifiers.

Aggressive reporters use other durable—sometimes dubious—techniques: secret taping of the unwary, reconstruction of an event long after it has occurred, use of undercover reporters, lulling the subject by faking note-taking or taking none at all. Appearing very sympathetic to tease out information. Reading memos on unattended desks, even borrowing them for photocopying. During a highly visible time for one company, the chairman's secretary returned to her desk to find a reporter with a highly confidential telephone log in his hand. The important lesson here is: Rather than argue, it is easier to be secure. Keep sensitive documents out of sight and accompany reporters while they are on the premises. Presidential Deputy Press Secretary Larry Speakes created an amusing piece of mischief when he left memos directly concerning press corps arrangements lying around on staff desks. The press found them and howled.

As Goldstein also points out, sometimes reporters just plain go too far. "They advise politicians, assist prosecutors, fabricate quotes and events, and, of course, make mistakes, then refuse to admit error."[23] One criticism of television coverage of the 1985 TWA hostage crisis was that the journalists seemed to be conducting diplomacy by network; they had become actors rather than observers.

Reporters cannot withdraw empty-handed. Nor can they fully understand an event without direct observation: seeing, smelling, touching, or talking to participants. Reporters themselves and their training pose other problems. Until Watergate, and to some degree once again, journalism schools did not attract the best and brightest. Working journalists tend to be young and inexperienced, first working on a newspaper well away from their home or college towns, and then anxiously moving on (and hopefully up) several times in quick succession. They have little time to fully understand a locality, or even a major subject, before they are off on a new adventure.[24] And one becomes a journalist when one declares it. Little formal control exists over the "profession"—no entrance requirements, no explicit or really enforceable code of ethics, and no system for weeding out incompetents and scoundrels. As Goldstein points out, even the U.S. Congress gave up attempting to define journalist.

Mistakes creep in through time pressures and differing interpretations of news. Editors can override reporters: most of the *Time* information damaging to Israel's Defense Minister Ariel Sharon was sharpened or changed in New York. (One young reporter had the weight of her words etched forever on her mind by such "sharpening." She had ridden in on a police officer's death. In writing the story's lead, the reporter carefully fudged the question of whether the gunshot wound was an accident or a suicide. An editor, unfamiliar with the case and without consultation, changed the opening paragraph and wrote the headline to read "suicide." The change was critical because of the police department's natural sensitivity to the issue of an officer taking his own life and the patrolman's Roman Catholicism. Later the patrolman's family came to protest the story. Much to the reporter's horror, his widow was a high school classmate.)

To be fair, some mistakes are difficult for a reporter to detect. Sources lie. People genuinely misunderstand each other. But reporters compound these problems when they do not try to understand or do not dig hard or deep enough for facts. The cardinal sin lies in deciding in advance what the story line will be and then finding the facts to fit the theme, or—as in the case of Janet Cooke's *Washington Post* "Jimmygate"—inventing them.

Newspapers are reluctant to admit when they are wrong or don't know. They equivocate, bluster, alibi, and hide behind technicalities, secretaries, or lawyers. Edward R. Murrow once said that the press does not have a thin skin—it has no skin at all. Although newspapers make a great fuss about running minor corrections—address, first name, or letters to the editors—more substantial corrections are rare. And they never catch up with mistakes. If made at all, the correction straggles in days or weeks later, usually in an obscure section of the newspaper.

How reporters precipitate events or watch immolation or other deaths is much discussed, more in the public arena than in business. In a recent case in Japan, the media sent out platoons, overwhelming the alleged mastermind of an elaborate scheme to sell bogus gold certificates. The press stalked him, waiting for something to happen. It did. He was murdered in his apartment while newspaper reporters and photographers jostled each other for a better peek through cracks around the door. They did not call the police. The incident created a great deal of soul-searching over the essential tension between being a human being and being a professional observer.

New Journalism, which burgeoned after Watergate—intermingling fact with fiction—complicated these problems further. Writers embellished quotes, burrowed into a character's interior thoughts, created scenes that might have happened but in fact had not, and made up characters who were composites of several people, laced with imagination. Some of the best-known journalists and novelists were involved: Thomas Wolfe, Gay Talese, Norman Mailer, Truman Capote, and Gail Sheehy.

The argument made by these authors was that since perfect objectivity is impossible, no choice remains in these either/or times but to abdicate to absolute subjectivity. The reporter became the center of interest rather than the real world he was supposed to be picturing or interpreting. Farther afield still, so-called "pipe artists" make up quotes and scenes.

More stringent editing and requests for sources, an ombudsman who adjudicates the aggrieved inside or outside the city room, and diminishing the star system would ameliorate these abuses. Attention must be paid soon. Studies consistently report that the media ranks very low in the public's confidence.

3

# Planning the Unplannable

## *Surviving Communications Crises*

A good P.R. program is like a guardrail on a cliff, not an ambulance at the bottom.

— Arlen Southern

WHEN kidnapping corporate executives was providing fun and funds for Latin American terrorists some years ago, a senior international executive, home from South America for a business meeting, asked his CEO what the company would do when he was kidnapped. The CEO, who looked as if he thought his trusted colleague had taken leave of his senses, replied, "Don't you mean 'if?'" "No, 'when'—it's just a matter of time."

Business crises are no longer a matter of if, but when; no longer the exception, but the expected—even the inevitable. Crises are more visible and severe, and arouse greater concern than ever before. They can damage—even terminally—a company and individual careers, and can produce interminable legal suits and government investigations that disrupt operations and the smooth running of a company for years. A more aggressive media, a volatile economy, weakening of respect for business organizations and those who run them, and unprecedented international competition should signal danger on any executive's fever chart. But like automobile accidents, the unimaginative think it will always happen to the other guy.

Reality may be sobering, but it still has not convinced some managers to think disaster and failure, not just of success. Many students who dissect why England succeeded as an empire would learn far more from studying why Spain failed, and still more from analyzing England's eventual imperial demise. Positive mindsets almost precondition a manager to fail because he does not know—much less imagine—what he will face. As a result he may find himself coping with an all-out disaster that he could have managed and contained when it was a mere disturbance.

Crisis planning is an obvious need, but surprisingly difficult to inculcate in a bureaucracy. Possible future concerns, which may never come to pass, deflect the time, attention, and priorities of busy managers who would prefer to deal with the problems staring them in the face demanding immediate resolutions.

Operating managers, trained in an immediate, pragmatic, can-do attitude, find planning for amorphous contingencies a mind-stretch. They find it even more difficult when forced to accept surprise, disorderliness, and the lack of a good, quick solution.

If the communications officer attempts to drum up interest in contingency planning, he is often put down as being a doomsayer or as trying to establish a power base for himself.

## Assessing the Risk

Risk and magnitude, visibility and liability vary enormously from crisis to crisis, from industry to industry. Some are self-inflicted wounds: tenders, plant closings, executives departing abruptly or staying too long. Others— plane crashes, oil spills, chemical leaks, and product defects—burst violently on a company.

Gerald Meyers, former CEO of American Motors Corporation, groups business crises into nine categories: changes in public perception, sudden market shifts, product failures, management succession, cash drain, labor strife, outside attack, adverse international events, and regulation or deregulation of an industry.[1]

Several factors escalate or minimize the risks. First is the quality and thoroughness of a company's preparation. Developing a philosophic base and a personal psychological gyroscope determines success infinitely more often than those eternally suggested checklists of opinion leaders, food service, and other basic how-to-dos, best delegated to staff. The Johnson & Johnson credo, for example, provided a shared foundation for action by all the executives involved in Tylenol recalls. Others gain objectivity and support from a circle of confidants experienced in crisis management. However, the ultimately more important is too often shunted aside by the easily organized.

The where, when, and who involved in a given event often determine the intensity and intelligence of media coverage. A plane crash on a remote Andean mountain peak, in which no Americans are killed, warrants a paragraph, if that, tucked away somewhere in the newspaper; the crash probably will not be mentioned at all on television, unless some spectacular pictures are available. Television feeds on dramatic shots.

But if the crash occurs near the commuter rush on the Fourteenth Street Bridge in Washington, D.C., with several prominent people aboard, television crews will flock in. Proximity of a television station and a film crew heightens the chance of coverage. So does the hour: close to the evening news. So do English-speaking news sources. The Air Florida crash in 1983 that occurred in just such circumstances illustrates how human interest aspects—a television favorite, whether the news is accidents, hostages, or corporate struggles—can obscure important news. The heroics of badly injured people struggling in the ice-caked Potomac River, others sacrificing their lives, and dramatic helicopter rescues pushed aside news coverage of possible faulty deicing of the aircraft's wings and other weak operational procedures during a heavy snow storm.

Air disasters also illustrate differing cultural reactions. When a Japan Air Lines plane crashed on a mountaintop in 1985, the company's president apologized in person to the families of the dead and offered to resign. The maintenance chief, after dealing with relatives of survivors day after day, committed suicide. Quite different behavior from that of the president of a United States airline, who might feel equally responsible and grief-stricken, but who probably would not visit the crash site, much less the families of the dead and the survivors.

Location also determines how much attention a crisis gets and for how long. When a major oil spill occurred off Santa Barbara, California, the news media and influential people—particularly fervid environmentalists—were nearby. Night after night, shots of ever-encroaching oil spills and birds, their feathers slicked with ugly black oil, were broadcast. No lives were endangered and within a year the ocean would have washed away the oil, but the pollution was made to appear life-threatening and permanent.

Who is involved matters greatly also. The Bhopal disaster was reported widely, but imagine the coverage if the tragedy had happened in Institute, West Virginia, which offers reporters relatively easy access, modest travel expenses, and no language barrier. Or conversely, imagine the coverage if it had been an Italian-owned plant in a remote area of Indonesia.

"When" weighs in exposure, too. One reason Union Carbide's continuing troubles gained so much attention was August. News holes—the space newspapers allot for editorial material—must be filled. When many good stories compete, some are sacrificed or cut severely. But in August, normally a slow news month, reporters must dig for stories. Hence Union Carbide's continuing saga was a godsend for reporters, who could milk a different aspect every day and fill space. So are hurricanes over holiday weekends and fires when the president is vacationing.

The news lull between Christmas and the New Year is another unfortunate time for the subject of bad news. In December 1983, Charles Z. Wick, director of the U.S. Information Agency and a presidential friend, was reported to have taped numerous conversations with major administration figures. Each day another aspect was reported; William Safire of *The New York Times* wrote several columns commenting on the taping.

Time of day and day of week influence coverage also, but less than many communicators hope. Releasing news just before deadline, on the theory that reporters will be too harassed to ask searching questions or do independent research, seldom works anymore. There's always a chance for a second-day follow-up. Once corporate communicators would release bad news late Friday afternoon. With the stock market closed the financial impact might be delayed or softened. And who reads the Saturday papers? Faultless in theory, but wrong. Surveys show that day, even season, affect serious business readership very little. And by Monday the *Wall Street Journal* will have fresh stories that have not appeared anywhere else. *Journal* readers willingly wait to read the financial and business interpretations.

The wise executive knows whether his operations and industry are high risk: extractive, mining, petroleum, and exploration companies; electric utilities (particularly those attempting to build nuclear plants), transportation, food and drug manufacturers, and chemical industries rate the highest. If media attention has already been drawn to an operation, particular care and sensitivity must be given to it. In 1985, when the press was watching chemical leaks and bank failures closely, it behooved any executive in these businesses to be absolutely sure his company was squeaky clean.

The most damaging crises are often concealed in deceptively routine occurrences: the most trivial, accepted events that pass unnoticed in the press of more important-seeming incidents. When the devil wears horns, he's not dangerous. You know exactly what you face.

Putting an incident in perspective when all around you are seeking sensation or seeing disaster is not easy, but essential. Frequent spills or minor fires in a factory, which the company knows are ordinary and unthreatening, may alarm a lay public and reporters, even if carefully explained—but surely if not.

Usually the early signals of trouble are ignored or played down, thus allowing the problem to reach a boiling point. Even when a crisis hits and goes public, insiders uncritically try to minimize its importance, to relegate it to a passing blip on corporate radar. One bank in serious trouble took the most leisurely route—mailing press releases even to important local newspapers—and said nothing at all to customers, employees, civic leaders, and financial analysts. Opinions were formed and the battle just about over before the bank's message was heard.

When the import finally is banged home, most executives react with impatience, seeking a quick fix, slashing at the Gordian knot. They may say nothing, overreact, or adopt a seige mentality.

The reasons to remain silent may be compelling within the company, but pose serious difficulties externally. Lawyers worry about the liability involved in talking. Sometimes there's disagreement about who should speak. And some executives are simply scared to face a hostile press for the first time. Others talk tough but carry a wet noodle.

Modern technology complicates crisis management. Machines supply an abundance of information—fast. Its very bulk and immediacy leaves no time for reflection or for broader decision making, and thus downgrades individual judgment. When facts, photographs, media, and peers all are clamoring for a decision, one must be made—hasty, incomplete, and incorrect as it may be. Imagine the CEO who responded to queries with, "I want to think about that."

Keeping your head while all around you are tense, afraid, or looking for the dramatic is key. So are careful, realistic assessments. Is the crisis created or deeply rooted? Will it fade away or escalate? Has the company done all it reasonably can? Should it stay in the fight? Or is it a no-win situation in which the company should cut its losses? One lawyer wisely advised his client to drop his suit, after he was involved in an auto accident. He had run a red light, hit a car containing three nuns, and the judge's name was O'Leary.

## Who Plans? After the Damage or Before?

Despite all the horror stories in the business news, many companies and their executives are still abysmally unprepared for serious trouble. Many palm off crisis planning to the communications department and then forget to ask what became of it. If the communicator pushes the project, he probably won't be listened to and will be ignored when the inevitable happens.

In June 1984, Western Union commissioned a study by Burson Marsteller Research to discover who plans, how and when, among *Fortune 1000* industrial corporations and 500 service companies.[2] About half the respondents (fifty-three percent) had plans, many established in the past five years in response to previous troubles. Industrial accidents ranked first among motivations, followed by environmental problems, investor relations (in some ways this ranking is surprisingly high), hostile takeovers, rumor suppression, strike notices, proxy situations, product recall, and government regulatory problems. Also mentioned by respondents were data communications breakdown, natural disaster, fraud or embezzlement, bankruptcy, and industry or service risks. Understandably, four out of five companies (eighty-one percent) handled crises themselves, although outside counselors may have assisted in the planning process.

Normally, planning is divided into two levels. The first involves noncatastrophic, usually local, often mechanical problems, such as water main breaks, commuter train breakdowns, or power outages. More extensive plans cover a widespread, sudden catastrophe—a large plant explosion, transportation accident, or bank failure—that must be handled with great urgency and speed.

Important as plans are, many are as desiccated as toy soldiers on a papier-mâché battlefield under glass in a museum. All the Sturm und Drang, the blood and personal pain, are drained. Such plans prepare a manager, psychologically or operationally, for a major crisis about as well as the recruiting sergeant prepares an enlistee for combat.

Among "important" details listed in the Western Union survey are: a phone index to reach key people twenty-four hours a day, travel agents, a twenty-four-hour food service, a laminated wallet-sized card of crisis team members, sufficient corporate news release paper and envelopes, potential press conference sites, and keys to all supply rooms. Important as these details are, they are routine mechanics, best left to support staff.

Battle-experienced managers and counselors aim for more extensive preparation and greater realism—even if simulated. Many plans do not fully prepare the media spokesperson or point man for leaks, incessant media barrage, disloyalty in the ranks, the emotional shock of damaging headlines, tapped telephones, defeat despite best efforts, and even death.

Some companies—but more frequently counseling firms—attempt to give managers a preview of such realities. Executives arrived at a consultant's office for day-long media confrontation training. Stepping out of their limos, they anticipated a genial oozing into the day. Instead, when they got off the elevators, they were besieged by a barrage of bright lights, demanding television reporters, and blocked access. The first lesson of the day—although play-acting—was searing.

Another executive had just survived a session of role-playing in handling industrial disasters. As he was packing up, the "widow" of a man supposedly killed in the accident called, blaming the executive personally for her husband's death and all the agony her family would face. The tough executive broke down. Brutal scenarios, but not unrealistic.

Untested managers aim to control crises; experienced managers settle for coping day by day, detail by wearying detail, hoping that all their planning, experience and their gut reactions will prevent a communications or financial disaster. Sometimes, the disaster lies not in the event itself, but in its public, media-shaped aftermath. Maladroit or unplanned company responses increase these risks—substantially.

## What Three Mile Island Taught

Two Hill and Knowlton officers have advised others and lived through their own share of crises. Robert L. Dilenschneider, president and chief executive officer, and Richard C. Hyde, senior vice president, counseled Hyatt Corporation during the skywalk tragedy in Kansas City and Metropolitan Electric after the Three Mile Island incident.[3]

Plan for the unplanned, they counsel, no matter how uncongenial that may be for highly structured organizations. Companies thrive on lack of surprises, orderliness, and chain of command. Crises are abhorrent because they break through unscheduled, unannounced, and often violently. Only with superior, realistic planning and execution, spiced with lots of luck, is there any chance to control damage. Sometimes adversity can even be turned to the company's advantage. The two counselors suggest four steps:

- Identify potential problems—existing situations, particularly those endemic to the industry, and past incidents that may recur.

- Identify affected audiences—employees, media, customers, government agencies—then develop appropriate spokespeople, messages, and actions.

- Organize a response team, assisted by written plans and checklists of contacts and actions. When a situation is chaotic and fast moving, this assures that subordinates will cover the essential steps. But the plan cannot be too rigid or specific; it must be flexible enough for executives to apply their common sense and experience to volatile situations.

- Make sure the company speaks with one voice—someone who is cool, level-headed, articulate, knows how the media works, and can make swift decisions, sometimes on insufficient knowledge.

Hydra-headed messages—conflicting stories from several people—not only confuse, but they may imply the company isn't in command, doesn't know what it is doing. All this is difficult when speed, tempered by accuracy, is paramount.

Conversely, mysterious silences, evasive answers, and absence of information only goad reporters to dig harder. Often they assume they'll find more detrimental news than appears on the surface. Alternative sources are available—always. One used frequently today is a financial analyst who follows the company or its industry. This is a good reason for keeping analysts well informed and favorably disposed toward the company. But there are risks. With fewer analysts covering more companies, their information may not always be fresh and precise—but they will never not answer.

The worst problem during the Three Mile Island (TMI) incident, according to the Hill and Knowlton counselors, was caused by the conflicting reports generated by overzealous media that lacked enough information. It was a technical story, difficult for the untrained to understand. In addition, nuclear terms in themselves often create fear. Confusion may be inevitable in such dynamic situations, but that's no reason for the company to contribute to it. "Reporters told us they really didn't know how to cover the story. It was difficult; technically complex; scary. Some reporters, frankly, did not want to go on location, fearing they would be exposed to radiation," Hyde explained.

But TMI posed other problems for reporters. First, television at best is an intrusive medium. Rural Pennsylvania, where the reactors are located, simply was not able to handle hundreds of media people and their equipment. Reliable information was scarce; facts kept changing. Reporters claimed uncooperativeness from the utility company, secrecy, and a confused federal bureaucracy. For all these reasons, and because of their lack of background, the press cut through the technical to focus on human interest—a technique that is overused and often abused. Not only does human interest sell newspapers, but it avoids the need to seek out the subterranean, complex issues that are much more difficult to cover. Reporting of the TWA hostage crisis concentrated on people and never explained the tangle of political, religious, and military rivalries in the Middle East that created the hijacking.

The Kenny Commission Report on TMI soberly concluded that the incident's risks did not warrant the hysteria and melodrama of the on-scene reporting. TMI was not journalism's finest hour.

The accident illustrates another media trend: narrowly focusing issues. In addition, coverage of TMI took the question of nuclear energy from the hands of specialists and bureaucrats and placed it squarely on the political agenda and in emotion-laden meetings.

Another crisis management problem is the poisoning of information wells. Phillip P. Fried, eastern public relations director for Monsanto Company, who has taught many crisis seminars and handled a share of his own, tells the following story, of another chemical company.

A tank car of vinyl chloride, derailed in a small Southern town, began to burn with acrid smoke. Civil defense people, after checking a manual, decided that burning polyvinyl would produce poisonous gas. They called the company's New York office to check this and to report that the National Guard was evacuating people in a twenty-five mile radius. What did the public relations contact advise? After checking with company scientists, he called back, assuring civil defense that the smoke posed no danger to anyone or anything. No poisonous gas would be produced. The civil defense people said, "Thanks for the assurance, but what about all the dead cattle around the tank car?" The company man could only wonder, to himself, if his own scientists had lied. When the stakes are this high, subterfuge among colleagues, politicking, or leaving the point man out there vulnerable to lie or respond with insufficient information only results in damaging headlines or serious community problems. Such strategies don't do much for corporate spirit either.[4]

Almost every crisis-experienced public relations practitioner has one cardinal rule, particularly when public safety is involved: Tell it all and tell it fast. Not only does this minimize fear because the general public is informed, but it means that the news makes headlines *once*. Dribbling out information disquiets people because they always fear that more and the worst are yet to come. Perhaps more damaging, this policy also drags out coverage for days, magnifying the event in the public's mind. Lawyers, financial advisors, and media-burned managers may disagree: "Tell the bastards nothing." "Stonewall them." One instance when silence was far from golden was when the Canadian Broadcasting Company accused the Canadian subsidiary of Star-Kist Food Inc. of shipping 1 million cases of "rancid and decomposing tuna." Throughout extended coverage the company kept mum. The result? They were massacred in the press. Profits plunged ninety percent. A brutal shock to Star-Kist and its parent H.J. Heinz, but totally predictable.

One besieged corporate lawyer sought to release as little information as possible to a very persistent, powerful investigative journalist. Colleagues urged him to answer at least some of the reporter's questions. He declined. Without benefit of any company cooperation, the reporter developed a story on his own, which appeared—to the company's detriment—on the very day they were wooing financial analysts.

Even more cynical executives say that if someone asks a question you think is out of line or not in your best interest, just plain lie. But this is not smart in the long run. As one business journalist explains: "I'm only human. They lie to me just once and I won't believe anything they say, ever again."

Faced with internal intransigence, particularly from superiors, the corporate communicator is left with the perilous choice of trying to convince the boss he's wrong, only to have a damaging story appear later. To press his point, the communicator may dredge up expensive war stories of how lying works only once and mortgages credibility, or how stonewalling and debating the public can unseat the most powerful, as it did President Richard M. Nixon.

However, telling everything may pose liabilities unless the company presents its case very carefully. Which phrases are natural headline grabbers? Which will confuse? Dilenschneider gives this example from TMI. A telephone company technician remarked that the phone lines might "melt down" because of call volume. The comment, a natural headline, was heard—garbled—and became the source of needless and ill-founded concern.

Hyde, who tussled with a multitude of communications problems at Metropolitan Electric because they were not prepared for the magnitude of TMI, suggests that the following factors be incorporated in any plan:

- Speak with one voice.

- Cover all bases, all important subjects to the fullest extent possible.

- Provide regular updates.

- Accept that in an increasingly technological world, a more complex society, more can go wrong.

- Understand that the less people know about what is happening, the more they fear the consequences.

- Get management involved early in crisis communication planning.

# Tylenol: A Credo Worked
# When Planning Couldn't

Surely few companies have had a crisis burst upon them with the speed, ferocity, visibility, and tragedy that struck Johnson & Johnson (J&J) and its subsidiary McNeil Consumer Products Company, maker of Tylenol.[5] In the fall of 1982, a still-unknown criminal poisoned the pain relief capsules with cyanide, killing, almost instantly, seven Chicago area residents.

Tylenol, J&J's single best-selling product line, in 1981 produced more than $350 million in sales and held thirty-five percent of the total analgesic market. With such spectacular successes, no company executive could imagine a cloud when Johnson & Johnson Chairman James E. Burke, just three weeks before the first death, asked his senior management to anticipate worst possible scenarios. What if something happened to Tylenol, he asked? It seemed almost an unnecessary question.

Individuals, in business or government, often cannot envision the ultimate horror. In developing scenarios for events in Iran when the Shah seemed all-powerful, for example, advisors advanced actions that could be controlled and managed—tepid extrapolations from what already was occurring. Their poverty of imagination—perhaps even of knowledge—prevented them from foreseeing the rise of a religious zealot, militant in his faith and in his opposition to modernization as exemplified by the Shah and the United States. In a similar manner, at Johnson & Johnson, imaginations did not stretch to cyanide-laced capsules and murder.

The case is interesting as a *success* story—unusual in public relations—and, even more, for the unique cooperation between press and corporation. It does not diminish these accomplishments or the complexity of Tylenol problems to point out that the company had everything to gain by the widest possible press attention as a means of saving lives, preventing panic, accomplishing a product recall quickly, and reasserting its outstanding reputation for product safety. These measures coincided with the media's need for the most accurate, up-to-date information that the company was gathering. The result was a much closer relationship with the media than J&J had traditionally maintained. In other instances to be discussed, where a company may gain less and risk more through complete disclosure, the issue of media relations is much less clear-cut and more controversial.

For some years J&J's corporate planning groups had included crisis management and disaster plans. Conventional public relations practitioners talk of lists, friends, and control systems. But to someone such as Lawrence Foster, Johnson & Johnson's vice president for public relations, who has survived a media firestorm, no crisis management plan could have coped with the Tylenol poisonings. Not even the best managers could have planned for a tragedy of such staggering proportions. Events were so atypical, unpredictable, and eruptive that instant improvisation was the only conceivable action. Devising or following a plan carefully sculptured beforehand was impossible.

Aside from the success of Johnson & Johnson's candidness and openness, the case is unique in the strength executives found in a credo developed forty years before by Robert Wood Johnson. The credo established the company's priorities and defined its responsibility to its constituencies. Such credos usually are treated like Boy Scout oaths: put on the shelf unread; honored but not heeded. J&J's provided a cohesive direction for decision-making, a solid footing when the sands seemed to be shifting dramatically almost every minute.

The credo looks deceptively simple and modern. Back in the 1940s, Robert Wood Johnson noted that institutions, public and private, exist because people want them, believe in them, or at least are willing to tolerate them. "The day has passed when business was a private matter—if it ever really was." George Cabot Lodge, in his *New American Ideology*, published in 1975, echoed this idea of consent, writing that companies can no longer continue to operate without the consent of their constituencies.[6]

Johnson listed four specific constituencies:

- consumers and medical professionals using company products,

- employees,

- communities where the company's people work and live, and

- stockholders.

He considered these guidelines as being not only moral, but profitable as well.

The Tylenol saga started slowly, with several press calls to the company asking about problems with the product and then reporting the first death at 9:30 A.M. (CST) on September 30, 1982. Despite the increasingly macabre news coming in from Chicago, despite the numbing disbelief, despite the horrible fear that someone had screwed up in the plant, calm decisions had to be made. The natural orderliness of corporate life was thrown into turmoil. It seemed like a death in the family. It was that painful and engulfing. As executives attempted to learn what was happening, they realized that the first stage of the company's response required methodical analysis, not shooting from the hip.

Almost immediately, the public relations staff, with management's total support, decided to cooperate fully and candidly with the news media. Only later was it realized the decision had been made without a meeting—a surprise, but a totally efficient action. Telephone calls from pharmacies, physicians, poison control centers, press, and panicked consumers began to pour in, as well as false alarms, crank calls, and good advice. One weary executive felt that he could manage the crisis, but not all the well-intentioned good advice offered by callers. Television and press coverage was staggering—eventually, 2,500 press calls, 125,000 clippings. It was the widest coverage given to any story since President John F. Kennedy's assassination. During the first eight days of the crisis, as much as twenty percent of one network's news time was devoted to the Tylenol story.

The damage was immediate. Within a few days the stock dropped seven points. Tylenol lost eighty-seven percent of its commanding market share in two weeks. Eventually, recall costs alone totaled more than $100 million, pre-tax, and the product reintroduction was expensive. (No exact amount was announced.)

As events progressed, several aspects became clear. Given the staggering levels of poison in the victim's blood, the cyanide could not have been put into the capsules in the plant, only at the distribution point. Although most interest, corporate and media, was focused on the immediate story, a wider concern was whether consumer trust in all product purity was jeopardized by mindless and anonymous terrorism. Were the benefits of self-medication at stake? The most routine everyday purchases suddenly seemed threatening. Even those who knew better hesitated before taking a Tylenol capsule. Copycat tampering was another general threat.

Early on, Chairman Burke formed a seven-member strategy group that included senior executives, those responsible for McNeil, the general counsel, and the public relations officer. They met twice daily to make decisions on rapidly changing events and to coordinate company-wide efforts. Their attention now centered on damage control and communication.

During the tragedy and in its aftermath, Johnson & Johnson established a number of communication vehicles:

- Toll-free consumer hotlines that, through November 1982, handled 30,000 calls.

- Full-page newspaper advertisements in major cities, offering consumers the opportunity to exchange capsules for tablets.

- Letters updating employees and asking for their continued support and assistance—which they gave, generously. Videotaped special reports for employees and retirees.

- Interviews with senior executives in major print and electronic media.

- Thirty-one million bottles of Tylenol were withdrawn and destroyed; eight million individual capsules were tested; eight bottles were tampered with; seventy-five capsules were contaminated. This massive effort helped convince the public of J&J's concern for product purity and safety.

- Television spots telling consumers that Tylenol capsules would soon return to the marketplace in tamper-resistant packaging.

- Every one of the 3,000 letters of inquiry and support was answered.

Following total product recall and public opinion sampling, the company decided to restore its reputation by fighting back against public paranoia and against damaging public images such as the television graphic that showed the product next to a skull and crossbones. J&J would stay with "Tylenol." A new name might suggest guilt. New packaging would be tamper-resistant in three ways: a sealed box, a protective collar on the bottle, and an inner seal.

Just six weeks after the first death, a second media blitz, this one a company-sponsored thirty-city press conference via satellite, announced the product's comeback and introduced the triple-safety sealed package. The media gave the story wide coverage, despite the death of Leonid Brezhnev announced the same day.

Not only customers, but the company and media seemed pleased with how the story had been handled—an unusual agreement. Editorials commented on a new level of corporate responsibility, on how a gap had been bridged between the news media and corporate public relations. The company was called candid and contrite, committed to solving the murders and protecting the public.

With government agencies, media, and business cooperating, two additional bottles of Tylenol capsules containing cyanide were returned, preventing other possible deaths. Most persons involved agreed that responsible, open public relations policies carried out at all levels helped minimize the spread of rumor and misinformation and provided valuable guidance to the public.

Chairman Burke had the first prescient word of warning about serious product difficulty and the word of summary: "When the public is watching carefully, they make incredibly smart decisions." The public had seemed eminently fair in assessing what had happened.

By early 1983, the product had recaptured almost seventy percent of its previous market share; eventually it regained the entire precrisis eight-five percent. Despite the enormity and visibility of the tragedy, Johnson & Johnson's image "as a socially conscious business remains undiminished." Nor was a single negative letter received from a shareholder, despite the fact that J&J's actions cost $100 million. Three years after this "antiseptic horror" the slayings remain a mystery.

In early 1986, Tylenol capsules were back in the news with another cyanide death. This time J&J made the dramatic and expensive decision to remove all over-the-counter capsules from the market. Chairman Burke was highly visible, explaining the decision on news programs and talk shows. But many persons were disquieted: another death, another serious breakdown of trust and this time almost overexposure of Burke in the media.

## Managing During Turmoil

In crisis situations a manager cannot have territorial imperatives and survive. One must trust and support with all available skills. The communication people must handle the news-gathering, the legwork, the drive for accuracy and completeness. The required analytical abilities, the eruptiveness, and the relentless deadlines reflect a newsroom ambience more than that of a corporation. But communicators must consult constantly with the legal department to determine what can be told. To whom? How can the company answer the newest charge? Operating officers involved must be asked for facts to confirm or refute charges. Senior officers must understand the strengths and weaknesses of certain public words and positions. Under pressure, the tendency is to take shortcuts, to exclude, but taking the time and effort to do the job completely avoids many surprises and costly mistakes.

Sometimes crisis management becomes a bit like walking through a minefield. Many corporate managers, particularly in communications, expect their responsibilities to be relatively risk-free. They ignore the risky underside of corporate life. When Earl Shoriss wrote *The Oppressed Middle, Politics of Middle Management, Scenes from Corporate Life* some reviewers condemned him as an enemy of business, and called the book "odd," provocative. Few accepted his tales of middle management misery, of fatal caprice, exile, secrecy, planned divisiveness, programmed fear, and toadyism.

Maybe some executives are fortunate enough not to have experienced such clammy frights. More likely they have been taught to forget. The few senior executive women sometimes are more candid in acknowledging the formless terror, exclusion, and ostracism.

To manage successfully in crises a manager must be prepared to deal with the dark and sometimes destructive underside. Distressing calls at midnight checking on media rumors. The accidental death of a very senior executive that arouses press suspicions—incorrectly. Many nights consumed by debriefing the brain of the day's events and preparing for fears of the next morning's struggles.

How can a manager be better prepared to fight a media firestorm? First, know how reporters work: understanding their needs, particular interests, biases, fierce competition, and relentless deadlines is basic.

Second, organize for turmoil as you would develop a strategic plan. This good mental exercise should never become an operational straight jacket.

Third, attempt to get mentally outside the corporate cocoon to view the company as others do. Historians are trained to bring as little of themselves as possible into an analysis or an event. Only if historians attempt to screen out the biases inherent in their late twentieth century purview and U.S. college training can they even begin to understand, for instance, the economy, strategic importance, and labor hardships of sixteenth-century silver mining in Potosí. Many executives, even with the best of intentions, view the world from a highly selective slice of experience, reinforced by peers who think the same way.

Fourth, be sure your house is clean and in order. If not, tell the truth up front. Concealment—which never works in the long-term—only heightens media coverage and skepticism.

Fifth, maintain a healthy personal balance, objectivity, and, if possible, a sense of humor and of the absurd. Stress, anger, haranguing the press or lecturing associates, great impatience—all endemic during pressure and turmoil—are self-defeating.

## Snatching Advantage Out of Disaster

Although downside risks must dominate a manager's thoughts and actions during a crisis, later he can use his experiences to produce positive results. Even executives who have suffered through tender fights and other assaults on their corporations admit that their ordeals forced them into long-overdue restructuring, shrinking operations—particularly of corporate staffs—and taking a very hard look at business actions shelved during more optimistic times.

According to Michael Tabriz, veteran of Love Canal, *Sixty Minutes,* and chemical industry public affairs, postcrisis analysis can produce the following advantages for the communications department:

- Elevating the public relations function. (In many companies it's looked upon as soft and fuzzy, not into the guts of reality—especially not in the face of trouble.)

- Focusing public attention on matters of critical concern and reaching audiences otherwise unavailable.

- Building credibility.

- Forcing an organization to review all policies relating to social responsibility.[7]

Conversely, big bucks and reputations can be made in crisis management. It's a hot ticket right now. Many besides communicators—lawyers, investment bankers, and outside specialists—are competing for the action. When companies are in deep trouble and need help, they often chuck conventional ways of doing things and hire savvy, tough street fighters, with lots of connections, documented successes in corporate conflict, authoritative auras, and a zest for battle. Even the language used—war rooms, scorched earth, raids and white knights—is martial.

Lawyers are becoming very adept at what was once the communicator's strongest suit: media relations. Lawyers grandstand their victories—Marvin Belli rings bells in his San Francisco law offices. A reporter likes nothing better than good copy. Lawyers talk with the press, sometimes daily, during a case, feeding background and other useful information. In a sense, many lawyers fight their battles on two fronts—court and press.

But, ultimately, the most dependable guides into the increasingly dangerous arena where a company's financial and operational future, even survival, may be at stake, are the executives who have overcome similar turmoil. Even their experiences, however, cannot be adopted uncritically as a surefire success. Despite some common elements, each high-pressure crisis is unique: the details always differ. In the end, a manager is thrown back on his own resources and those he develops under pressure.

# 4

# Supplying Your Own
# Banana Peels:

## *Troubles Companies Cause*
## *Themselves and Others*

Authorities ought to know that a careless word can bring down the
greatest empire.

—Ryszard Kapúscinski

DETECTING burgeoning crises, planning for the most common varieties,
then managing these somewhat predictable emergencies all take the
measure of a manager far more than eruptive disasters that come zinging in
totally unannounced. Rather than "merely" a matter of facing an awesome
problem at hand, self-generated problems create battles and dilemmas within
each manager. He must respond with self-examination and skeptical fore-
sight, battle rigid priorities and natural optimism, and suppress the urge to
hide or to falsely explain away problems. Successful managing of either type
of crisis depends upon the quality of media relations, the CEO's and spokesperson's credibility, and whether the problem is acknowledged or hidden.
The following three chapters focus on the analyses of communications in individual cases—some generic and others prominent, some successes and
others expensive disasters.

Even in supposedly objective organizations personalities still can dominate
and damage. It may be a woman executive—new, alone, and vulnerable in
the executive ranks—who does not understand that appearances can decide
more than facts. A CEO may court unnecessary liabilities and criticism by
being very visible and available—as Warren Anderson of Union Carbide at
Bhopal—or absent during disaster—as William J. Catacosinos of Lilco during

a massive power failure. Public announcements of senior management arrivals and departures usually are sanitized into personal reasons or other business pursuits: cover-up illusions as revealing as the emperor's new clothes. But often power fights go public. The boss won't leave—Harry Gray of United Technologies—or won't let his heir take change—Harry Gray, Harold Geneen of ITT, and Dr. Armand Hammer of Occidental Petroleum. Or the company creator hangs on until he is pushed out, as in the celebrated battle between Steven Jobs and John Sculley for control of Apple Computer. Communications strategy in these cases is a Hobson's choice. There is no clear-cut satisfactory solution. The risk of making enemies and inflicting long-festering wounds is great. Sophisticated, patently bland explanations arouse skepticism and curiosity about the unrevealed real reasons. But airing corporate dirty linen and personality conflicts in public has liabilities also.

Most of the troubles that companies cause themselves, however, spring from not monitoring operations closely enough for possible public liabilities, trying to hide wrongdoing even when it is uncovered, then stonewalling or lying to the press. Managers who would consider it reckless to present a business plan without solid marketing, financial, competitive, and legal research, neglect to factor in public considerations. At other times a company takes the public rap when others are more culpable, as Hooker Chemical Company did at Love Canal.

Sometimes reason dictates minimizing the possible effect of well-based or ridiculous rumors. But rumors can seriously damage banks, as Continental Illinois learned, sadly, and Manufacturers Hanover, positively. Procter & Gamble had to pay the devil his due to quell an off-the-wall rumor that their products were doing the devil's work.

Under supportive and innovative corporate leadership and when allowed to work as it should, communications produces successes. Federal Express is one example. Not only is it a market winner, its business language, planning, and colorful public image is strong, exciting, and contemporary. More often, peers in management kiss off communicators as hip shooters, unable to produce profits or long-range plans. The public relations-created Cabbage Patch Kids craze proves the contrary. Perhaps it was too successful: demand far outstripped supply, creating another communications problem.

Communications expertise can assist in explaining the necessary but painful realities of shrinking markets, closing operations, and laying off longtime, loyal employees. An example of the successful cooperation of labor, community, government, and corporation is Amfac's closing of a Hawaiian sugar plantation.

But the most profound self-inflicted troubles are the great games of tenders and mergers played by white knights and raiders. Many such corporate wars founder on less-than-candid communications and cultural conflicts. The melding of INA and Connecticut General into one still-floundering, not-yet-profitable insurance giant, CIGNA, illustrates these pitfalls—particularly in promising employees too much and later terminating them in the name of cost-avoidance.

## When Appearances Create Reality

Business and journalism alike pride themselves on being fact-driven, on solidly grounding their decisions on statistics and hard information. In reality, appearances—accurate or misleading—may be decisive. What people believe—fact or fiction—dictates their actions. Why else would disinformation be so successful?

Perception gaps should concern any senior manager. The public and media often act on what they see or believe, which is not necessarily the truth. Women executives—still few, very visible, and vulnerable—ignore appearances at even greater personal peril than male colleagues. Not fair, but the reality. Understanding this power of appearances and media interests could have drawn much of the sting and attention out of the celebrated, overpublicized Mary Cunningham–William Agee–Bendix Corporation brouhaha. One contributing factor was giving the media a news peg, thus freeing reporters to print what previously had been only rumor. Also, leaks from dissident directors, fired executives, disgruntled competitors, and family kept popping up as snippets in gossip columns, even in business reporting.

Cunningham, despite her Harvard MBA, was naive in her understanding of how others would perceive her zeal for strategic planning and her relationship with male colleagues—particularly her mentor, Agee, at that time Bendix's CEO. He escalated the risks by promoting her to too much power too soon and by putting her in the greatest flack-catching position in a company: vice president for strategic planning. Even under ideal conditions, planning is extremely sensitive; it redirects markets, kills off products, suggests sale of subsidiaries, and enhances or downgrades careers. At Bendix, the appointment was inflamed by Cunningham's age, sex, attractiveness, business inexperience, but mostly by her perceived relationship with Agee.

Cunningham showed her contempt for communications from the very start. She yearned for the guts of operations. She did not want to be "sidetracked" into writing or rewriting Agee's speeches, although she did this and far more menial chores. She wanted to steer clear of public relations or personnel—admittedly a ghetto for corporate females—but accepted the vice presidency for corporate and public affairs when Agee offered it to her.

Her media problems started locally, when a *Detroit Free Press* reporter asked, "Isn't it unusual for a woman like you to be in so high a position?" Cunningham thought he was referring to her academic background—a major in philosophy and ethics. Agee made matters worse by commenting to her, "Don't worry about him. He is just an ass. He doesn't mean a thing." Any business executive that far off target—not understanding what the reporter was asking—is in for trouble. Good or bad, giving any member of the media short shrift, the brush-off—particularly a hometown reporter—is dumb.[1] Conversely, treating even the friendliest member of the press as family, a kindred spirit, or attempting to philosophize when all the reporter wants is facts immediately courts difficulties. Too much proximity and access are risky. Allowing a reporter from *Fortune,* or any other publication, to spend days with interviewees, as Cunningham and Agee did, although highly desirable for the writer, is a potential mine field for the subjects. Few persons can be disciplined and guarded hour after hour, particularly under great business pressure.

Most public relations people urge companies to tell all, fast, but this counsel has downside risks. Spokespersons must carefully watch what they say, must be sure the information is complete and honest, and must consider as many ramifications as time and deadline pressure permit. Often an innocent quote today is later recycled out of context. Bendix fell into all of these media traps.

Damaging press coverage was triggered by Agee's "Western candor" at a routine annual meeting with Bendix employees. (Some press reports gave the impression this was a special meeting called to clear up Agee's personal situation.) He commented, with invited press present, that "Mary is a very close friend of mine and my family." The appropriateness of this comment to employees, press, or board of directors is debatable. What is not is the news peg created by the statement and the license it gave the press to write publicly about what had previously only been a private matter.

A Bendix public relations manager had advised addressing the issue publicly and had encouraged inviting the press to the meeting. This advice prompted Gloria Steinem to ask Cunningham later whether the manager was a friend. Steinem, understanding the importance of appearances very well, commented: "I hope to God that you . . . are having an affair, because you're sure paying the price for it."

As the drumbeat of press coverage intensified, Agee and Cunningham encountered picture problems. They learned that pictures can lie and mislead. One, taken at a business meeting, was cropped to appear as if they were gazing into each other's eyes. Another, in *People,* showed Agee on his knees before Mary sitting on their bed. These instances illustrate the classic mistake of not thinking critically enough about an event when photographed, much less how the picture will appear in print to those unfamiliar with the situation. Dirty tricks in photographs – airbrushing, cropping, taking people out or putting them in, even total faking – change meaning, sometimes completely. But that's nothing new. Fabricated photographs have been around a long time. Some of the more infamous tricks include Charles A. Lindbergh parading past the Arc de Triomphe in 1927 (he didn't), posed models, duplicated events to supply shots photographers had missed, even superimposed heads. A sensationalist New York City tabloid ran a "picture" of Rudolph Valentino entering heaven. Usually, photographs are cropped or airbrushed for vanity or as gags, but some alterations have serious political or personal implications.

Another tactic is taking a picture that clearly tells a story – but falsely. Ron Nessen, press secretary to former President Gerald Ford, cites a picture taken of campaign chairman Rogers Morton looking bleary-eyed and dismayed in front of a batch of empty liquor bottles and beer cans. Reporters had helped consume the booze, but the photograph gave the impression the "Ford campaign was drowning its sorrows."[2]

The print media were reveling in "Executive Sweet" and "Bendix Abuzz" stories. Such attention is to be expected. Outsiders invest corporate executives with power far beyond the realm of what's reasonable. When an attractive, highly placed woman appears in this predominately male preserve, it is rare – great news. Finally, the more easily understood and salable reports of human interest, mergers, tender and ego battles push aside the mundane and difficult to understand stories on finance and operations. A journalistic Gresham's law dictates that spicy news pushes out the sound and sober.

In her account, *Powerplay,* Cunningham notes that "things surged ahead with the inexorable speed of events that precede something very good – or very bad. . . . We were actors being asked to read increasingly more difficult lines – but someone else was writing the script." Not completely; in their maladroit handling of media relations, the principals were assuring unsympathetic coverage.

Naively, she still hoped the attention would subside. Naively, she trusted Gail Sheehy, who had interviewed her at length three years earlier for *Pathfinders.* The best reporters, and the most lethal, act as confidants and friends.

During the brouhaha, Sheehy called, assuring Cunningham that she knew what an ethical, honest person Cunningham was. Even though burned and wary of the press generally, Cunningham still agreed to a twenty-minute interview. Sheehy also talked for half an hour with Agee, alone. When her five-part series, syndicated nationally in newspapers, was about to appear, Sheehy again assured her subject that it was business-like. "Don't worry. It's very sympathetic. You'll love it." However, Sheehy had pulled deep background information from the confidential interview for *Pathfinders:* alcoholic father, dead brother, upbringing by mother and a Roman Catholic priest. The story incorporated pop psychology with what Cunningham noted were many inaccuracies.

One of the great strengths of *Powerplay,* a cautionary tale for any corporate man or woman involved in intense media visibility, is the vivid description of the overwhelming pressures of having every word and action reported upon. Of being recognized everywhere and harassed in person and on the telephone. Of hiding. Most corporate leaders are essentially very private people—some almost shy—operating in a very protected, orderly world. The cold bath of public exposure shocks and bewilders—always.

Even after Cunningham resigned from Bendix, explaining that "unusual convergence of events beyond my control has substantially impaired my ability to carry out my responsibilities as a corporate officer of Bendix," the "vultures and voyeurs" were active. Even her ninety-one-year-old grandmother was approached. Life became corporate soaps. No article on Bendix, even in respected business publications, was complete without titillating references to Cunningham. But she also invited more comment and coverage by such actions as going for a prolonged retreat with Agee to his Idaho home. By the time Cunningham gave her well-received Commonwealth Club speech in San Francisco she and Agee had both learned to field questions more adroitly. Neither wanted to create any more media events. When Cunningham was discussing her childhood and music preferences with a WQXR host, she spoke with the extreme caution of one badly burned by exposure. Agee became gun-shy even on relatively routine corporate matters.[3]

However, caution did not prevent the couple from embarking on another highly visible corporate adventure that was bound to excite more press coverage: Bendix's attempt to acquire Martin Marietta. This produced far more drastic consequences for Bendix and for Cunningham and Agee personally than had the media circus surrounding their supposed relationship. Any hostile merger invites great risks as well as great rewards. Concentrating on financial and legal aspects while ignoring communications increases the risk, which is precisely what Bendix did. The major appearance mistake, however, was including Cunningham (at this point Agee's wife and a Seagram vice president) in merger meetings. Dick Cheney, veteran tender and mergers specialist for Hill and Knowlton and Bendix's outside public relations counsel, warned how damaging her presence could be. She was not a Bendix employee; the press would focus on her participation, and she would stiffen the machismo resistance of Martin Marietta management. She went.

This merger battle, which ended with the independence of Martin Marietta, the absorption of Bendix into Allied Corporation, and Agee losing his job, illustrates several communications weaknesses. Cunningham lists three distinct press-generated impressions. First, that she functioned as a Lady Macbeth, whispering evil stratagems into her husband's innocent ears. (Actually, her very appearance at meetings was more damaging than any advice given.) Second, that Bendix was a big, bad wolf out to gobble up poor harmless Martin Marietta for its own greedy ends. (It certainly looked that way, although Martin Marietta was far from harmless.) Third, that what Agee did during the whole ordeal was bad for business, bad for the country, even bad for the American way. (Whether to buy assets rather than create them, or to pour millions into mergers rather than produce products is a question troubling many executives and economists.) "All three are neat and tidy apothegms, but untrue," Cunningham concludes.[4]

She views herself and Agee as victims, scapegoats. She is still angry that people deserted them, people whom she feels should have known better than to swallow the media point of view. The press, she writes, forced a false personality and history about her, one she was forced to defend or counter, again, and again, and again. "Being blind-sided . . . shakes your confidence to the core," she wrote. You become paranoid: looking for reporters and photographers everywhere. Maybe that's realistic, reminiscent of a poster popular some years ago that read: The fact that you're paranoid doesn't mean people aren't out to get you.

The media—and its audiences—likes nothing better than simple stories and simple tags for prominent personalities and complex situations: Alexander Haig as arrogant, Rosalynn Carter as the iron magnolia, and Harry Gray of United Technologies as the finisher.

Like Cunningham, many persons would be much more comfortable if the press admitted to being a business that operates with the same rules and the same profit and loss risks as any other commercial enterprise. In the media's world, "If it's true, that's nice, but if it sells, that's even better."

Trial by media makes private concerns and vendettas public, pressures and intrudes upon individuals, and may focus on the dramatic at the expense of the important. The challenge for those involved, particularly communicators, is not to feed the press exactly what will produce the dramatic but damaging headline or story; to accept that the relationship can never be one of family or philosophizing. For women—caught in the double standards of executive suite and media coverage—ignoring appearances, particularly with their male colleagues, invites pain, misunderstanding, unwanted attention, and often business defeats.

## Egotism: The Victorian Secret of Business

In his book *Managing,* Harold Geneen, former CEO of ITT, fingers egotism as any corporation's hidden, most costly disease. It is far more damaging in dollars and effort—particularly for the communications department—and to public perceptions, yet is far less acknowledged than alcoholism. Any manager with a drinking problem, no matter how senior or important, will be confronted by the liabilities of his illness. Not so with egotism, which remains as hidden as sex was in Victorian lives.

Egotism demands a heavy price of communicators. The sensitive relationship between communications officer and his senior management, often based more on chemistry than on demonstrated accomplishment, and his role as conduit to the public, make him the most vulnerable manager in the company. One counselor who has helped many fired executives says a CEO's megalomania, which intimidates subordinates and distorts reality, prevents him or his company from taking full advantage of public relations. Such managers may say they want to be told the truth, he points out, but they either damage, demote, or dismiss the bearers of such truths. They begin believing their own public relations, discounting a contrary word from the press or anywhere else. They seek personal stature even at the expense of the company.

Symptoms of egotism are highly visible, rampant, and expensive. The countless and costly printing charges involved in producing that vanity piece of the company, that albatross of any communicator—the annual report—is just the tip of the narcissistic iceberg. (Although the annual report serves many audiences—financial analysts, shareholders, potential employees, government, and community leaders—internally it too often evokes sheer ego. Who is pictured? Whose operations are featured?) Prestigious speaking opportunities before peers, press, and politicians; memberships in the Business Roundtable or New York Economic Club; doctoring photographs; transforming internal publications into family albums; all the pomp and panoply of office are symptoms, too. Airbrushing photographs is expensive. No matter. Cover the chairman's bald pate with hair. Take out the wrinkles. Put a more attractive head on the president's shoulders.

A few war stories follow that document the extent of the disease. Many will smile and say, "I don't do that." "Amusing, but that doesn't happen here." Just wait and look.

Woe to the trusting communications officer who thinks all is resolved when annual report photographs are agreed upon. Second, even third guessing is standard operating procedure. One annual was delayed to assuage an executive's wife, who was angered because her husband's picture was not scheduled to appear. The result: another photography session, redesign of several pages, delays, more costs, and the soothing of egos of peers not pictured. Another communications officer relates the nightmare of senior executives demanding extensive changes on blue lines—the last process before printing. This money- and time-consuming procedure dramatically increases the risks of costly mistakes and delays. Regardless, the executives haggled over every comma, every "the" to "a" change, the size of signatures, until, in despair, the communicator began assigning arbitrary, expensive price tags. Want to remove that comma? It will cost fifty dollars and one day. The running tally soon reached a staggering amount, almost as much as the total estimated printing budget. That finally quelled the rampant egotism.

Another communicator suspects that he got his job on the strength of his possible ability to secure a peer-generated invitation to the Business Roundtable for the chairman. But perhaps the apogee of ego is captured in this incident, recounted by a Washington-based public relations counselor. A client CEO asked if his daughter could meet the president the next day while she was in Washington working on a college political science paper. Facetiously, the counselor asked if the daughter would like to lunch or dine with the president. The response: "Gee, that's great. I'll ask my daughter. If her schedule permits either, I'll call back."

Media relations and internal publications suffer from executive egotism, too—an ever-growing appetite as addictive as any narcotic. When Thomas McCann presented the coup of coups—a long, positive *Fortune* story—Eli Black was dissatisfied; he wanted the cover. In Black's zeal for maximum publicity, he transformed United Fruit's internal publication into a family album dominated by his photographs, cover paintings by his wife, and spreads of his visits to company operations and of his cavortings with Central American dignitaries—a classic ego trip. Nothing undermines a publication's credibility and usefulness faster than its use as a personal ego prop or as a platform for the company's position, with nary a nod to employee concerns or interests. A recent corporate vanity, *The World of Armand Hammer*, is 255 pages of Occidental's chairman pictured with movers and shakers, the perks and props of power. *The New Republic* called it "executive porn," part of the gray-flannel fantasies that business publications feed their readers.

But executives tend to forget that the more visible they make themselves, the more they grandstand corporate financial strengths and cultural contributions, the more vulnerable they become. Everyone wants to topple the big-mouth.

George Reedy, in the *Twilight of the Presidency*, relates the dangers of ego-feeding and isolation in high office. His thesis: office neither elevates nor degrades a man. Rather, it provides a stage upon which all of his personality traits are magnified and accentuated. Egos, Reedy writes, must face daily clashes with similarly strong peer egos. Must pay obeisance to reality. Must cultivate an environment where fools can be called fools. Where sycophants can be duly observed, discounted, and weeded out. Where a devil's advocate can be encouraged, since no man is wise enough to play his own. This is difficult because high office prevents even old, trusted friends from telling a leader "go soak your head." Certainly Reedy did not feel free to say that to his long-time associate Lyndon Johnson once he became president. We have become fearful, Reedy concludes, of disputatious personalities and clashing ideologies. The press is the only external uncontrollable force that can tell the president what is really happening, and even the press does not enjoy the free exchange that it once did.

---

## The P/L of CEO Visibility

The risks and advantages of high visibility and personal involvement bedevil any CEO and his counselors. Crises only raise the stakes.

Although everyone initially applauded the concern and caring that Warren Anderson, CEO of United Carbide, demonstrated by flying to the scene of the Bhopal tragedy, others question whether it was in the best interest of anyone—Anderson, who was arrested by Indian authorities, or Carbide, which tied its corporate presence directly to the disaster rather than localizing responsibility in its subsidiary. The chairman may have confused his reactions as a person with his responsibilities to the corporation.

One aspect of visibility is crystal clear. Vacationing during a crisis or flaunting perks while pleading tough economic times are symbolic disasters that court trouble—always, as the chairmen of Lilco, Amax, and other companies are learning painfully.

Hurricane Gloria hit Long Island hard on September 27, 1985, knocking out power for thousands of Lilco customers. Even as late as October 7, 1,000 customers still lacked electricity. Where was the utility's chairman, William J. Catacosinos? Vacationing in Europe, where he lingered until October 3. He attempted to save face at a press conference upon his return. He admitted that the hurricane damage was the "worst catastrophe" the community had experienced, but he praised Lilco's preparation and response as "outstanding." He contended that company officials handled the crisis smoothly in his absence and explained that he maintained close contact with them by telephone. "I came back at the appropriate time to assess the situation." But not to salvage his image as an executive sensitive to symbol as well as substance. Responding to a reporter's question later, he conceded that he had erred in not returning sooner to direct efforts to restore power.[5]

Catacosinos' delayed return allowed company-threatening problems—financial weakness, political criticism, and the licensing of the Shoreham nuclear power plant—to escalate. The company, near bankruptcy in 1984, omitted its dividend for five consecutive quarters. Long Island politicians praised the dedicated efforts of workers to restore power, but roundly blamed management for delays. One local leader spearheaded a costly campaign to transform Lilco from a privately held utility into a public power authority.

When the hurricane hit, some legislators were already opposing the federally supervised emergency preparedness test required by the Federal Nuclear Regulatory Commission before the Shoreham plant could be licensed to operate. Management of Shoreham's construction had also been criticized. Maladroit handling of public concerns quickened the criticism.

Public takeover discussions emerged again early in 1986, when Governor Mario Cuomo and New York State Republicans and Democrats, in both Senate and Assembly, supported a state takeover of Lilco. Another group with 8,000 members proposed to accomplish the same aims by creating a new power authority to acquire Lilco's stock. Some criticized the company as one of the worst managed in the country, with rates among the highest in the United States—and predicted to go still higher. Others sought alternative sources of power and called for mothballing Shoreham or preventing its opening.[6] All illustrate a colossal lack of community support. Perhaps all of these problems and critiques would have surfaced eventually, but knowledge of a chairman vacationing while many of his customers on Long Island coped with darkness and cold dinners gave anger a focus and a thrust.

Absence or concentration on the trivial to the neglect of the important are symptoms of executive malaise or incompetence, but they are often excused or covered up. Many executives immerse themselves in do-gooder activities or long quasibusiness trips to retreat from intractable problems in the office. Or, like Captain Queeg of the *USS Caine*, they worry extensively about who ate the strawberries rather than why their ship cut its tow rope. When such actions have hardened into patterns and intransigence, no solution short of departure is feasible.

Very obviously flaunting abused senior-level perks, while others are losing jobs or having their careers blighted, discourages the sacrifice necessary for corporate survival. Golden parachutes and bonuses in spite of poor financial results are easy targets for media and stockholder criticism. Other companies teach economic realities, unwittingly, to their detriment. One large corporation simultaneously announced the closing of several mines and the purchase of an expensive jet to ease executive travel to company facilities. Another insensitive manager rented a stretch limo to reach a factory to announce its closing. Still another in a rather confined business community tooled about in his chauffeured Mercedes while red ink flooded the company's financial statements and he was wooing bankers for understanding. Awarding large executives bonuses while workers are being exhorted to sacrifice for the company's survival or just before filing for bankruptcy erode employee loyalty. Quite different from Lee Iacocca's exhortation to share the suffering.

Absence, controversial decisions, and high-handed actions are imperiling another CEO—Pierre Gousseland of Amax. He was vacationing in Corsica when Amax announced it would lay off twelve percent of its workforce, including a large part of the headquarters staff—those most aware of Gousseland's whereabouts. A director bluntly told Gousseland to spend less time out of the country.

Gousseland also has "galled insiders and outsiders alike." Despite long-standing financial problems, Amax only recently sold its Newfoundland fishing camp, available to executives, and put its two Colorado condominiums on the block. Amax policy prohibits executives from flying first-class, even on Atlantic crossings, but in 1982 one of Gousseland's corporate favorites was rewarded for being the most frequent user of the Concorde, whose fares are usually double first-class.[7]

And two Amax planes still fly. Something in the psyche of young nations and imperial corporations needs a symbolic airplane. But they can be very expensive transportation, no matter how well justified from an operational point of view.

Senior managers normally lead very private lives, avoiding or having little contact with the press and other publics until elevated to leadership. Their introduction must be carefully coached and planned. Too early a debut may reveal a natural (but possibly a hobbling) incomplete grasp of all operations and the new role. Too late may diminish the appointment's news value. Too much publicity risks overexposure and prompts questions of why the touting or ego trip, or who's minding the store. Too little raises questions of hiding and squanders the value of people's natural identification with individual managers rather than structures, and keeps financial analysts and others from studying the new executive. Managers often vacillate—hesitate to go public while fully understanding the need. Some eventually get hooked on visibility. To be effective, the communications officer must effectively plan, orchestrate, and balance conflicting needs and demands, and ration appearances to best serve both the executive and his company.

## The Chairman Goes to Washington

Managing amid corporate turmoil can begin with a single announcement. When President Jimmy Carter nominated Textron's chairman, G. William Miller, to head the Federal Reserve Board, the company's relative normalcy was transformed into a maelstrom of events, tensions, and investigations. The microscopic, almost engulfing volume of attention from national media, government agencies, and financial analysts thrust the corporation, its management, and its operations under a magnifying glass.[8]

Sudden extensive national attention paid to any company produces surprising ramifications—magnification of flaws, flaunting of well-stated policies, and exposure of weak individuals—that even the most seasoned managers can scarcely begin to imagine.

Even before the official announcement, Textron's telephone switchboards lit up like Christmas trees. The media attention was extensive and constant. More like tough reporters than a corporate staff, Textron's communicators did a great deal of legwork: checking out rumors and constantly attempting to release as much information as was necessary and possible. Media people were in the company's offices, on the telephones, seemingly ever-present with more questions. Who was Bill Miller? Did his speeches give any clues to his possible positions at the Fed? Later, questions got tougher. Who paid what to whom for helicopter sales? Who knew about it, when? In all their responses, communicators stressed Miller's well-known and frequently announced policy of absolute honesty in company dealings.

A few less-than-professional journalists snooped around the offices, rifling through papers on secretaries' desks and creating a need for tighter security. Few executives had experienced such high-intensity press attention; they questioned why the media always seemed adversarial. Information revealed during confirmation hearings before the Senate Banking Committee and in the media resulted in four independent investigations by the Internal Revenue Service, the Justice Department, the Securities and Exchange Commission, and a special committee of Textron's board.

Perhaps a way to recreate the tension and eruptiveness—more like a newspaper city room than a corporate department—is to share some of the headlines. It started gently. The *Wall Street Journal* asked, "Bill who?" then waxed euphoric in a combined corporate-personal profile headlined:

> Golf Carts, Buses and Operas
> G. William Miller
> The Amalgam of Superman,
> Solomon and Sir Galahad

Other early headlines were equally complimentary: "Known for skill and public service." "A decisive corporate humanist." But the early bloom soon faded. The headlines began saying: "The Senate digs deeper on Textron's payment in Iran, slowing Millers' track to the Federal job." Each morning, managers were happy not to see Textron's name emblazoned in headlines—the reverse of the usual PR practitioner's dream of visibility.

Textron's executives—already stretched by responding to investigations and allegations, a new management team, and adjustments to great visibility—were confronted in December, 1978, by an international crisis: Iran. Bell Helicopter-Textron, then the largest U.S. employer in Iran, stayed on the longest with the most people. In addition to its concern about getting six to seven thousand Textron people out safely, the company had contractual obligations. Investors and analysts were worried about how the loss of Iranian business would affect Bell's earnings. Because of the chaos, the press was getting very little information and much of that eventually proved to be false.

One morning, shootings were reported at the Hilton Hotel, the embarcation point and sanctuary for Bell employees. Some senior executives allegedly had been captured. Fortunately, both stories proved erroneous, but the truth didn't reach Textron for many anxious hours.

Dominating Miller's nomination process and the Iranian crisis was the pound, pound, pound of vast numbers of telephone calls, the sheer volume of complicated, delicate questions to be answered and the constant surprises. But those two years of battle-like pressure honed a cardinal principle about crisis coping. Most of the major events that hit Textron in 1978—Iran, Miller's two presidential nominations, and the subsequent investigations— were external and largely unpredictable. And Textron is not alone with that problem. Time pressures and demands on senior management force them to focus on internal operations. To balance this corporate communicators must act like a corporate radar, spotting specks on the horizon—today almost imperceptible, but potentially of serious concern to the company. Then, most difficult of all, they must convince peers in senior management of their seriousness, and anticipate consequences, both predictable and imagined.

## When the Boss Won't Go

Few corporate creators are as astute as Roy Little, who left Textron, severing all formal ties, including his board seat. It was not fair, he explained, to look over my successor's shoulder, to second-guess. An imaginative entrepreneur, Little developed new and profitable interests in venture capital and start-up companies.

Such graceful, planned exits from power are relatively rare. It is very difficult to leave your company—psychologically akin to leaving a child—in someone else's hands. If the former CEO remains on the board, unusual sensitivity and trust are required to make the relationship work. Often a person with the entrepreneurial, inventive skills essential to creating a company cannot refine operations and plan long-range—as in the case of Apple. The entrepreneur usually follows a single, even solitary trajectory. Lyle M. Spencer calls him "the wild man in an organization," who doesn't want to be bossed around.

Some CEOs, like Harold Geneen of ITT, harpoon a successor with hidden agendas, informal power, and criticism until he is pushed aside completely, but only after battles are fought in newspapers. Others, such as Harry Gray of United Technologies, are accused of attempting to harass selected heirs, again causing embarrassment for the individuals involved and the company (in UT's case for the directors as well). Inventive fathers Steven Jobs and Steven Wozniak of Apple were pushed out in highly publicized battles. All these antics leave the public, stockholders, and employees wondering who is tending the store. Both winners and losers lose publicly.

Each struggle over succession has important communications components. Given the colorful, dominant personalities involved—good copy for the media—it is difficult to control public damage, short of muzzling everyone involved.

Harold Geneen unwillingly surrendered his CEO title in February 1977—forced to step down after bitterly fighting the board's decision, according to his biographer, Robert J. Schoenberg.[9] The action was surprising on two counts: the early dispatching of Geneen and Lyman Hamilton's selection as CEO. Geneen agreed to continue as chairman for about a year to give Hamilton the benefit of his experience.

Publicly, Hamilton was hailed as a favorable development, a big plus for ITT. The press was sympathetic, writing that Hamilton was apparently taking hold and tidying up the structure. Actually, he had three strikes against him almost before he came to bat.

Geneen did not want him—or anyone. Publicly he was self-effacing; privately, he barely tolerated what was happening. Also, ITT's structure and operations, its mixture of businesses and their management, were designed in Geneen's image. Some felt that only he could run the hodgepodge of nearly unmanageable ventures he had concocted. And the former CEO retained enormous unofficial power among some staff, directors, and media.

As Hamilton assumed more control, differences deepened. Where his predecessor was growth oriented, Hamilton aimed for profitability. He began selling off what he considered to be business dogs, many of which had been Geneen's pets. The street and financial analysts had long experienced difficulty understanding the incomprehensible agglutination of 250 disparate businesses. Hamilton decided to conform operations to the five groups used in public explanations. As the sniping and meddling continued—much of it public—Hamilton began suspecting Geneen loyalists everywhere.

And then, in July 1979, Hamilton was fired. Most observers agree that the board would never have acted without Geneen, aging, shorn of power, devastated, even humiliated by the ITT board, but still able to tower over and influence the rich and powerful. Hamilton's apparent acceptance belied power dynamics.

Rand Araskog, Hamilton's successor, was freed of Geneen's presence, only to face many of the same business and public problems as Hamilton—plus a new one. He, too, struggled to transform a museum of investments and management ideas from the 1960s into a more nimble, modern, technology-centered company. The profit machine, run to produce ever-increasing quarterly profits with scant regard for the long-term, was slowing down.

Araskog faced two important communications problems. First, he penalized the messenger who bore news he did not like to hear. Executives interested in survival soon altered their presentations to the way he liked them. And Ned Gerrity, one of the most powerful public relations practitioners and a confidant of Geneen, was suspended; he then left amid reports of an internal investigation into leaks to press and shareholders, particularly on the question of divestiture.

With a floundering giant and a relatively new CEO, another problem arose: possible takeover. Myron Magnet of *Fortune* explained the dilemma:

> Antagonists in takeover battles don't always look like armies marching into an open field in glorious formation, drums beating and flags flying. Often they act more like dogs circling their prey in the woods at night, driving it back and forth between them, while the alarmed target, with teeth and claws of its own, can't be sure if the dark shapes it sees are shadows or substance.[10]

Was Geneen still in one of the shadows? Possibilities of takeover, divestiture, softening results, problem subsidiaries, and public disagreement all leave ITT with the chore of rekindling a positive image with the press, who once wooed the company as its darling.

Similarly, the qualities that helped Harry Gray build United Technologies—forceful, flamboyant, dominant, and great acquisitor and finisher—stymied his relinquishing of power. Edward Hennessey was heir apparent until he left for Allied Corporation. Then, Robert Carlson acquired the mantle, only to resign suddenly after publicly acrimonious displays. He charged that Gray had wiretapped his home and office. A board investigation, extensively reported in the media, uncovered no evidence of improper actions. When Robert F. Daniell became president and CEO, Gray continued as chairman, with no announced retirement date. Public and embarrassing board room fights; the selling off of one of Gray's prized acquisitions, Mostek; and the new CEO may spell greater caution and prudence for both business and communications.[11]

Without a doubt, the most public and most widely reported power struggle between founder and successor was the shoot-out in Silicon Valley between Steven Jobs and Steven Wozniak—who began Apple Computer in a garage—and John Sculley, brought in by Jobs to run the highly successful business.

Jobs, who had built Apple into a *Fortune 500* company, felt forced out by his hand-picked CEO—and said so in many interviews. The youth of the computer industry, Silicon Valley's boom-and-bust nature, and the intensity with which people develop and market new technology breed nasty disputes, sudden departures and fights over trade secrets, inventions, and market advantages. But Apple's internal battle was particularly nasty—and very public.

Charges flew from both sides. Sculley claimed that Jobs tended to value technological elegance over customer sales. That his intense involvement with the MacIntosh project had demoralized other Apple divisions. And that he ruffled feathers on staid Wall Street—and among East Coast folks—with his brashness and overbearing self-confidence. But Jobs' troubles also illustrate a generic problem. His vision, drive, charisma, and his relentless championing of the personal computer had made Apple a success. However, these skills seldom transfer into the more mature stage: a structured company, a competitive environment, and long-range planning. Even his early collaborator, Wozniak, questions whether Jobs could put anyone's interests ahead of his own. Communicating such attitudes, no matter how obliquely, creates a morale problem.

Sudden, dramatic market changes, which made it plain that Apple would have to be more largely structured to survive, caused the crucial rift between Jobs and Sculley. Management style had to change also, but was the shift more apparent than real?

When Apple was riding high, "event marketing"—extravagant corporate announcements that reaped lavish press attention—were standard operating procedure. With a less successful business story to tell—rushed reorganization, twenty percent of the workforce laid off, the first-ever quarterly loss, and a stock low—Apple sought less publicity. Unfortunately, through most of 1985, coverage was corporate soaps. Turning off the publicity hype once so arduously sought is difficult when business goes sour and the company prefers not to talk.[12]

Only in very unique situations and through unusual relations with the press is such silence possible. Thomas Ross, senior vice president of corporate affairs for RCA Corporation, explains this problem and his success. In 1982 when he arrived at RCA, top management was absolutely chaotic. There had been four CEOs in ten years, politics was rampant, and morale was at rock bottom. The company was overdiversified and overextended.

However, Ross had advantages: a CEO who understood the press and took the spokesman into his confidence. Second, almost everything bad about RCA had already been written—many times. But, perhaps crucial, Ross, once a journalist himself, knew and was respected by many in the press and broadcasting. Even so, persuasion carried more weight than contacts. Ross argued that more stories about RCA would only bore readers, be terribly repetitious. He appealed for a breather, promising to open doors wide when the company became newsworthy again. After getting the corporate house in order and conducting research that indicated RCA had a neutral image, the company resumed its public presence, first with corporate advertising. The theme: "RCA: one of a kind."[13]

Although many other companies, such as Apple, might wish to emulate this success, RCA's and Ross' positions were unique. Nor did RCA's problems invite the high drama of the chips warriors.

Initially, Jobs and Sculley looked like an unbeatable combination—a deliberate visionary and a driven corporate type, but good friends. Soon they differed on almost everything from authority to board instructions. What signaled to one a phase, the other saw as a reprieve.

Eventually, when Jobs left the company, it had been damaged by public squabbling, threats of resignations, and rumors that filled information gaps. Little was explained publicly. With Sculley firmly in control, it was hoped the company could present one face to dealers, customers, and others. Many business prospects had been put off by the turmoil and conflicting messages from rival leaders and product divisions. Although Sculley imposed new controls, pared Apple's bloated operations, and said he wanted to build the company in his image—cool, disciplined, orderly, and driven—ego reared its head again. When Sculley presented Apple's 1986 plans in San Francisco, they featured a multimedia slide show, twenty-two-city teleconferencing, and a specially written rock theme song, all presented in front of a huge blow-up of John Sculley.[14]

Will Sculley echo Jobs' public image, but without his enterprising and inventive drive? Even the settlement with Jobs was a joust of public relations people speaking for the silent principals. Job's representative explained that Jobs was happy to put it all behind him. Apple's public relations firm, Regis McKenna, in a prepared statement, said that the settlement protected the shareholders.

Perhaps all of this high drama and amusement in Silicon Valley and the computer industry made good copy. But more conservative investors, financial analysts, customers, and shareholders would be attracted to a less turbulent image, and an orderly transfer of power.

# 5

# Assets Don't Talk to Assets

## *Merging People and Cultures*

The optimist brings his lunch on Friday.

—Corporate folk wisdom

MERGERS are rapidly becoming the corporate equivalent of war. The jargon and zeal are martial: raiders and white knights, poison pills and war rooms. Greenmailers and buccaneers strap on their six-shooters to prey on flabby, unsuspecting managements.

Joseph A. Schumpeter, an Austrian economist best known for his studies of business cycles, views such creative destruction as natural, even essential. Capitalism can never be stationary. In Schumpeter's terms, the realistic capitalist, rather than seeking to administer existing structures, studies how to create and destroy them. Others see tender-merger spurts as part of a business cycle from entrepreneurs and founders to professional managers to institutional investors and savers. T. Boone Pickens notes that by the early 1980s, American industry was no longer a money-making machine. Many companies were too large and too inefficient. Managements had lost their edge or were doing too little work. Current turbulence has unseated many a manager who once thought he was entrenched for life.

Business unrest has also expunged many once-venerated corporate names: Conoco, Kennecott, CIT Financial, Sunbeam, Standard Brands, Seven-Up, INA, Connecticut General, Salomon Brothers, and Anaconda, among others. The dying is often very obvious and painful. One morning I noticed workmen removing the large bronze Girard Bank nameplate from the patrician headquarters in Philadelphia. The Girard name—long venerated for the man, Steven Girard, and the school and bank he founded—was erased by the purchasers, Mellon Bank, from all offices and a major plaza in Center City.

As long as resources—plants, products, and companies—are cheaper and more exciting to buy than create, variants of corporate raiding will dominate managers' lives and communications. High visibility, megabucks, and great ego trips accorded to the winners only encourage the great corporate wars to continue. Many question how productive these company couplings are, but not why they founder: underestimating the human factor and conflicting corporate cultures. One senior executive involved, not entirely happily, in an acquisition said, "They forget assets don't talk to assets." Even a merger that looks good on paper will fail if people don't trust each other, or if they feel the other side is taking over more battles and positions.

Cultures in conflict can be deadly serious, but also humorous. General Motors, Hughes Aircraft, and EDS are an odd threesome. The footwear of choice and the chairs tell the story. At General Motors, scientists and engineers wear traditional black brogues; at Hughes, sneakers; at EDS, even shoes with buckles or tassels are outlawed. At GM's Allison Gas Turbine, gun metal gray desks and chairs are crammed against each other and institutional green walls; at Hughes' modern, almost plush facilities, engineers sit at computer terminals in ergonomically designed chairs. Another stumbling block arises from regional stereotypes: the views outsiders hold of natives of the Midwest, California, or Texas, for example. Conflicting attitudes also can be a problem, as when people with a no-can-do attitude come up against free spirits willing to tackle anything.

Jones and Laughlin and Republic Steel literally were on opposite sides of the river—and much else. Their computers didn't talk to each other. Different terminology and business systems created other inefficiencies. In truth, both of the former entities are dead, except in the mind lags of employees.

Gulf's merger into Chevron, touted as the perfect match on paper, in reality was very difficult. The relatively posh Gulf offices in Pittsburgh, with personal secretaries and considerable managerial autonomy, contrasted with Chevron's austere quarters in San Francisco, with crowded secretarial pools and complicated systems even for something as simple as requisitioning material. Many in Gulf's management were outsiders in contrast to a majority of home-grown executives at Chevron.[1] In another company, even the process of press releases created problems: one communications department popped them out without fanfare, the other wrote clearance procedures often longer than the release itself.

Communications plays a major role in helping or handicapping a tender offer. Richard Cheney, chairman of Hill and Knowlton, has been in the thick of many battles—with T. Boone Pickens, Marathon vs. Mobil, and the Carrier case.

In discussing Marathon, long a Hill and Knowlton client, Cheney cites reports in the media that compared Marathon to a jiujitsu wrestler, using Mobil's weight against it. Marathon energetically emphasized Mobil's size, its well-known desire to obtain oil cheaply, its high public profile, and its perceived to-hell-with-them-all attitude. Marathon's executives and 2,000 employees at its headquarters in Findlay, Ohio, worked hard to stir up the greatest public outcry ever against Mobil's takeover bid.

Marathon's eventual success may seem a bit surprising. Mobil's legions of experts appeared splendidly equipped to fight a public relations battle, but Marathon's guerrilla campaign was highly effective. In fact, it may have even strongly influenced the court proceedings.

The Carrier case, to Cheney, illustrates another rule of takeovers: fight to win with every argument and action at your command. If you have home-town strength and support, as Carrier did in its ultimately unsuccessful struggle with United Technologies, you can attract public attention, stiffen management backbone, and boost morale.[2] Raymond D'Argenio, Cheney's opponent, agrees that communications played a central part in UT's tactics. The acquisition was not entirely amicable; he explains it was fought in the streets of Syracuse. Opposition was spearheaded by the Chamber of Commerce, quickly joined by the local Catholic bishop, a group of ministers, the city council, the small business council, the local congressman, the Sheet Metal Workers Union, The United Way, state legislators, county officials, the media, the Junior League, and just about everyone else with clout in the community. Cheney, he recalls, was always somewhere in the background of the fracas.

To counter this, UT's chairman made himself available for questions and answers from the local press. Had we hunkered down and avoided the media, D'Argenio explained, we could not have gotten our side across. UT also combated dark rumors swirling about Syracuse that they were a bunch of corporate rascals in Connecticut. Television people asked to visit UT. They toured plants, flew in a UT Sikorsky helicopter, talked with employees, and lunched with, then interviewed Chairman Harry Gray on camera. In Syracuse, UT's chief financial officer spoke to analysts; press people talked straight to the media. According to D'Argenio, reporting changed gradually from hostile to balanced and even friendly to UT's point of view. Legal and communications departments coordinated efforts, so that the company could stay on the offensive with well-timed salvos. In sum, communicators were part of the company's top strategy team, working closely with financial people and lawyers, writing their own press releases (instead of farming them out to a counseling firm), and being accessible to the press. And, "we were plain lucky."[3]

More companies are better prepared to put up a good fight than they might think, Cheney comments. Once you decide a takeover attempt is not in the stockholders' best interest, you cannot neglect any weapon. Each attack requires its own strategy. There are no set rules. If you resort to dirty tricks, Cheney points out, the odds are overwhelming that you will soon be discovered and lose the day. Cheney himself uses only materials in the public domain—often his adversary's own statements and filings—which he assembles very carefully as background to interest reporters in a story.[4] In addition to the easily recognized, insidious costs of a public battle, there is the risk that aggrieved employees or members of the former management will bad-mouth the company.

Not only communicators but some lawyers consider talking the key in takeovers. Martin Lipton, a senior partner at Wachtell, Lipton, Rosen and Katz, explains that lawyers have their reasons and bankers theirs for not talking, but any deal "has a life structure of its own." The structure involves how two companies communicate with each other. How do they cut a deal if one doesn't want it? Most counselors advise that, if a company wants to remain independent, it should say so, loud and clear, unequivocally. Otherwise, rumor alone can spark interest, where there is in fact none.

Bendix failed to consider communications and psychology in their unsuccessful attempt to take over Martin Marietta. Instead of the CEOs talking, a letter was sent to each director saying, in essence: I control your corporation. Instead of sensible communication covering the essence of the situation, the Bendix management decided they had a legal edge. They tried for a purely legal victory—and lost. Lipton concluded that "people in charge of communications should run corporations."[5] Little chance of that in the near future.

---

# And Then There Was
# One Floundering Giant

Although trace lines of change can be detected in slower-moving, less-secretive situations, mergers such as that between the insurance giants INA and Connecticut General, now CIGNA, usually burst upon all but informed insiders. Mergers may dominate the corporate milieu and be much bruited about in the press, but your own merger always shocks and surprises. Like a death in the family.

In 1980, INA represented solidity, tradition, and more than a century of successful operations. The elegant colonial and Georgian headquarter buildings dominated one of Philadelphia's beautiful main squares and European-style boulevards. The hushed, lush ambience of the executive floor, the original art, symbolic silver inkwells, old fire engines, and other Philadelphia memorabilia—the sense of class spelled continuity. But one fateful decision to merge with Connecticut General turned the structure into the shell.

The rationale was faultless. A merger of equals. The companies were mirror images of each other: INA was essentially entrepreneurial, property/casualty, and international; Connecticut General was more process-oriented, known for life and health insurance, and strong domestically. In theory, the volatility of the property casualty cycle would be softened by the more predictable, actuarially driven health and life insurance operations. Together, the two companies' almost $12 billion in sales would be safe from other raiders.

Given the current business climate, most managers are likely, at some point in their careers, to be immersed in mergers, takeovers, and other bewildering, formless, unpredictable situations. A merger usually looms secretly and comes swiftly. Secrecy is essential for legal, morale, financial, and many other good reasons. But when only a few in the inner circle know of the merger, it gives them great power. They can plan the company's and their personal futures much more profitably than someone lower in the organization—even vice presidents, who become pawns of shock.

The individual officer is left to prepare for the unpreparable with little solid information. He must identify his audiences, friends, and possible enemies; develop strategies of when to fight and how; and seek a few experienced guides, who will prove invaluable. The situation he faces is amorphous and unique, requiring very specific yet flexible strategies. Tactics may change daily, as givens constantly shift. Even senior executives are plunged into a heady, frenetic, and exhilarating situation, a crucible where careers and companies are at jeopardy. Their lives will be in the eye of the hurricane for months. Relationships begin to assume the nature of plots for power and alliances to win or—more often—just to survive. The penetrating glare of high visibility and media attention sharpens these problems and relationships.

Secrecy is a great burden. Before each comment, before each assignment, an executive must ask himself if an individual knows or can be told. Because the communications department deals primarily with external audiences, a mere whiff of hesitation or fear can be easily detected by trained company watchers and perhaps hyped to the detriment of the individual, the company, or its shareholders. The communications staff must be told what is essential to know soon enough to prepare themselves psychologically and to develop the necessary press releases, but not so early as to breach confidentiality.

They day of the INA–CG announcement, emotion and future concerns were submerged by the immediacy of activity. Joint announcements to the press, local community, and employees were followed immediately by a New York City press conference. Spokespersons were prepared privately for the tough, searching questions that reporters would ask them publicly. Such a briefing is probably the most delicate, perilous role for a communications officer. In the euphoria of the moment, most executives are fervently convinced of the rightness and soundness of their decisions, hence are not inclined to take advice. Any negative thinking is dismissed as disloyalty, of not being a team player.

When the media hones in on weaknesses or confusion in public statements by executives, it's too late. Thinking on one's feet is not always wise when every word is weighed and reported on. Many heaped scorn on President Eisenhower for his tangled syntax at press conferences. They were confounded to learn that early in his career he wrote speeches for General Douglas MacArthur, who was known for his grace with words. In interviews after his presidency, Eisenhower was "surprisingly" articulate. The answer is quite simple: Eisenhower learned to carefully weigh his public utterances.[6]

Initial reaction to the insurance merger was euphoric. The press called it a merger made in heaven with enormous potential, a shrewd effort to squeeze out rising costs. The financial analysts applauded also. Not a discouraging word was heard on Wall Street. In the hubris of the moment, guarantees were given to the headquarter cities, Bloomfield, Connecticut, and Philadelphia, and to the employees that would return to haunt the leaders when cost avoidance emerged as the dominating goal.

---

# I Guarantee You . . . Cost Avoidance

The guarantees given to employees illustrate the danger of saying too much, too soon. Initially, INA's CEO, Ralph Saul, said, "Not only will it [the merger] not have any adverse effect on jobs in the Philadelphia area, but over the long run it will have a positive effect." Later, Saul said, "Ninety-nine percent of the people will stay right where they are." The story soon soured. Newspaper headlines began to read: "Layoffs begin of a magnitude almost unheard of in the insurance industry, but were called 'absolutely necessary' to cut expenses and save $40 million in 1983." And next: "Company gives generous payment; hopes to retire some additional employees as layoffs continue." And a final quote from Saul, "If we could get it through people's heads that one of the reasons for the merger was cost avoidance. . . . After all, we are running a business."

There were many pitfalls in attempting to strike a balance between promising employees too much too soon and saying enough honestly to quell fears and premature, costly departures. In such situations, some managers retreat into silence. Others leave communications vacuums for fears to fill; give hydra-headed, confusing messages; or stress legal, financial, and structural aspects at the expense of people. Also in CIGNA's case, drastically different corporate cultures were generally ignored, except by employees, who circulated a cartoon showing two armies falling on one another—INA, a howling horde of Huns; and Connecticut General, a mechanized, orderly mass.

One of the undiscussed, sometimes disconcerting challenges of mergers is to manage essentially three structures simultaneously: that which was, is, and will be. Announcement of a merger—even an unsubstantiated rumor— changes the existing organization, irreversibly. The charts may stay the same, but the dynamics and the power are very different. Everyone is scrambling for new, expanded turf or fighting fears of job loss or demotion.

Between announcement and consummation, the structure is subtle, perhaps not even consciously acknowledged. No one really knows where he or she fits in or what the outcome could be. It's difficult to keep equilibrium or perspective. This period can be productive—even creative—but it can also detour, dismay, even defeat some managers.

Meanwhile, a third organization is evolving to meet new demands, power realities, and personalities. Even a senior manager may have very little influence on what happens to him or to his department. He may not even know what is being planned or being driven by the process itself. Rumors fill information voids. Shifting people to different jobs, relocations, demotions, and layoffs create morale problems that internal communications and assurances from supervisors can only partially mitigate. Decisions often appear whimsical, unjust, and unnecessary.

The melding and crunching of the two insurance giants demonstrates many communication opportunities, some overlooked at great cost by

CIGNA. First was a name search. The aim was to incorporate the initials of both, first as North American General, until the acronym NAG was recognized as pejorative. Finally, CIGNA was selected. The headquarters seemed to be on a helicopter halfway between Connecticut General in Bloomfield and INA in Philadelphia. New York was halfway house until Philadelphia eventually was chosen.

Senior staffing was like ordering from a Chinese menu: one from column INA and one from column CG. The dual CEO seemed to work at first: Ralph Saul of INA was Mr. Outside, handling government affairs and public presence; Robert Kilpatrick of Connecticut General was Mr. Inside, running operations. Their apparently complementary skills seemed necessary to accomplish the myriad tasks of merging. Early on little friction was evident between the two men. They were always interviewed together and pictured side-by-side in pink chairs. Later, difficulties between them would surface dramatically.

Eventually, the press began to criticize what they had once touted. "They're trying to control a ship in a storm with two captains and two crews who don't know each other." Also, the first management shuffles began, in preparation for the merger that became a Darwinian struggle for survival and clients. Employees became victims of the much-heralded synergism. Ten percent redundancy was declared, and 4,000 jobs were purged by the end of 1982. A nation-wide, five-day, forty-six-city road show attempted to sell the shakeups and quiet fears.

To bolster employee morale, there were more pep rallies and merger newspapers. Employees reflected the reality more accurately, however, through clandestine cartoons and "please fire me" letters to local newspapers. Shuffle, shuffle, and change continued. Employees worried about the veracity and dependability of what they were being told. Outsiders were plainly bewildered. The vitality and life were draining out of what only eighteen months before seemed like a cornerstone of Philadelphia. Listening to executives' war stories, a senior public sector officer confessed, "I believe you, but I don't believe it."

Merger euphoria evaporated quickly. On April 18, 1982, a financial analyst meeting put the "stocks on skids." From a postmerger high of 55⅜, the stock slid to the 40s after the analyst meeting, then continued down during 1983 to the high 20s. Wall Street judged events harshly. "After premature analyst meeting, maladroit pitch and poor first quarter results, stock price slides." Others critiqued the CIGNA presentation as: "Vague, unfocused, less than straightforward, no solid information;" "no speaker mentioned current results;" "didn't have their act together, have a credibility problem." Merger costs—$14 to $15 million more than anticipated—surprised management.

Even so, CIGNA ran a merger announcement advertising that quoted the once-ecstatic comments of financial analysts, Wall Street, and the press. New corporate advertising mutated the once cerebral, problem-solving tone into huge photographs showing apparent guerrillas with bandoleers slung over their shoulders, titled: "Not all corporate takeovers are the result of winning a proxy fight."

Aftershocks continued, mucking up the merger made in heaven. Key executives, mostly from INA, began to depart, led by John Cox, the very visible head of INA's property casualty company. Eventually, Ralph Saul went, leaving Robert Kilpatrick in full charge. Their bitterness surfaced publicly. "This isn't a fallout of the merger, but a very orderly transition that will give Mr. Saul the chance to put his feet up and take it easy for a few months," the new, sole CEO said. "Mr. Saul stepped out of management really a year ago. The Chairman's role has been a very part time job for us."

Saul explained, "After forty years as a working stiff at various kinds of institutions and then ten years here, I'm really going to pause and think about what I'm going to do."

Other problems continued: Employee firings and voluntary departures. Loss of market momentum. Personal futures suddenly loomed far more important than corporate activities. Few new products were developed. Earnings declined eighteen percent the first year and more steeply later. The press and Wall Street soured: "Wall Street mistook future potential for present profit." "It's a case of corporate indigestion." "There was entirely too much optimism." "No experienced executives are left to solve the massive property casualty problems." "The struggling giant seems to be floundering." Huge underwriting losses reached a record $1 billion in 1984. Two sales told the story poignantly. Early on, Saul saw the potential in insurance companies widening their financial services. INA bought a position in Paine Webber. After the merger, CIGNA's twenty-four percent position was sold. Also, INA's headquarters and tower were sold for $135 million, with a thirty-five-year lease-back agreement.

How was the public assessing the merger? A *Fortune* article, "Help, My Company Has Just Been Taken Over," by Myron Magnet, noted the Darwinian struggles and how paranoia reigned supreme. Connecticut General discovered that its new partner wasn't all that it was cracked up to be. Many said that they got less than they had bought. Another former officer said "the multitudinous and whimsical" management changes did not produce the management wattage needed.

CIGNA purged 4,200 people, the majority from INA. Morale scraped bottom. The quality of work suffered, as did CIGNA's financial performance. As the miracle marriage became an odd couple, the press began to ask: "Who's in charge?" Prosperity turned into scrimping. The emotional integration will take years.

Today, CIGNA has a mixed communication challenge. On the positive side, it can position itself as a strong firm, innovatively marketing insurance as a constellation of employee benefits. However, it must overcome publicly the decanonization and disruption of the equity, credibility, and operational history that INA enjoyed and must return to profitability.

Managing communications during a merger teaches many things – indelibly.[7] First that, by their very nature, mergers burst swiftly and unexpectedly into one's life. Secrecy becomes power. Layers and loyalties that once seemed so solid and so clear, become rooted in quicksand. Everything will be magnified, inflamed, and often appear amorphous. A manager will experience conflicting loyalties between being upfront and honest with subordinates and adhering to procedures and messages agreed upon by superiors. Lying may produce a short-term advantage, but it destroys credibility in the long run. Employees will sacrifice if they feel they are being treated equitably and honestly, or – as Lee Iacocca says in his autobiography – feel they are "sharing the suffering." A manager forgets at his peril that strong, volatile, even destructive emotions are involved when someone's employment future is at stake.

Executives, tempered by corporate change, know the dangers of initial euphoria among colleagues, the media, and the financial community. Everyone is excited by the idea of a new or larger company. There's a great deal of macho thrill in acquisitions and tender fights. But, if the financial and other promised results are not produced in the long-run, those wonderful kudos will turn to very sour criticism. Some messy recent mergers are creating even initial skepticism. Veterans of corporate turmoil agree that an executive can never be completely prepared, but if he ignores the communications aspects, or handles them maladroitly, the results are guaranteed to be expensive.

# 6

# Eruptive Disasters
## *Of Accidents, Leaks,*
## *Fires, and Deaths*

A SINGLE telephone call reporting a chemical leak, an industrial accident, an airplane crash, a skywalk collapse, or a nuclear meltdown can entangle a corporation in a maelstrom of public exposure. Even handled well, such crises are expensive in management time, reputation, and dollars; mishandled, they court disaster, even corporate death.

Some eruptive disasters can be sensed, but not always, even by sensitive, intelligent, intuitive managers. Realistically, the best any senior executive can hope for is that each individual within his organization will be resilient and intelligent enough to slog through wearying, discouraging, tense days, which always last longer than anyone ever thought. There will be moments of anger and frustration when the media, even colleagues not in the trenches, protected by all the wisdom and knowledge of Monday morning quarterbacks, will carp, criticize and second-guess. Colleagues may attempt to use the inevitable mistakes, even essential personal visibility, against individuals involved in the crisis—particularly those in media relations. A plant manager taught not to discuss company policy publicly or to refrain from press statements is in a cruel bind when his plant blows up. Even if he handles the media well, he may be criticized; should he louse up through inexperience with reporters, or be accused of grandstanding, he may find himself a sacrificial scapegoat.

Bureaucrats do not like surprises. In times of quiet they can act smoothly and effectively. But when conflict breaks out, peacetime managers must be replaced by crisis leaders—a painful, although necessary, sorting out. The formal organization chart may or may not change, but power and respect shift.

The greatest trap for executives attempting to anticipate or cope with eruptive crises is the eternally optimistic can-do attitude prevalent among Americans. Young men recruited by spit-and-polish Marine sergeants and raised on John Wayne-type heroes, who always won rather painlessly, were stunned by battle-field realities in Vietnam. Wayne's heroes had taught them to expect easier victories. Corporate battles are little different, although the pain may be more psychological than physical.

The eruptive crises to be discussed here all illustrate important communications points. Bhopal raises questions of CEO visibility, cross-cultural communications and management, the absence of a communications representative, liabilities of hobbling media relations and stonewalling important reporters.

Most airlines accept the possibility of a crash someday, and therefore have carefully developed crisis plans readily available. Although airline accidents usually are rather narrowly focused in terms of time and location, and the procedures relatively repetitive crisis to crisis, managers in other industries can benefit from the airlines communications planning.

Many executives are stunned when their company's good reputation becomes a powerful magnet for adverse attention. Alfred Geduldig, president of Chester Burger and Company, sees the press, cans of spray paint in hand, anxiously waiting to cover the cleanest corporate wall with graffiti. Good relations with the press or various other constituencies offer scant protection when scandal hits. GE and E.F. Hutton have learned that even white hats get hurt; General Dynamics found doing what everyone else did in the defense industry was little defense when the rules changed.

---

## Love (Canal) Isn't What It Seems

In literature we have been taught to wince at George Orwell's cynical use of a word to express the opposite of its normal meaning. In history, the late Fernand Braudel, luminary of the French Annales School, analyzed events on two levels: the surface—easily seen and understood, dramatic and fast-moving—contrasted with the almost hidden and difficult to comprehend, the mundane and slow-moving. The first level may be obvious, but the second is far more important and decisive.

Love Canal illustrates these ideas, as well as how the media can exaggerate and inflame, particularly when the company involved plays pussycat or stonewalls initially. Fads and hot causes, whether whipped up or real, must be dealt with. It really does not matter in such instances if something is true or people merely believe it to be so, the result is the same.

Ironically, the site of the future chemical dump was named for an ambitious entrepreneur, William Love, who envisioned building a huge hydro-electrical project in the Niagara Falls area. He produced an environment dramatically split between the spectacular natural beauty of the falls and the "tired industrial workhorse," "a festering blister of the Industrial Age."[1] Complicating the community's adverse reaction to industrial blight was its dependence on industry, particularly Hooker Chemical Corporation, for jobs. Tourism could not take up the slack.

Love Canal became widely known as a chemical dump whose seepage created panic among nearby residents and wide controversy about culprits, causes, and controls. On the surface, Hooker, once owner of the site, was the great public villain. Less recognized as responsible were U.S. Army dumping, the local school board's role, panic inciters, the self-serving actions of some government agencies, and a symbiosis between environmental extremist scientists and scoop-seeking journalists.

The conflict is supposedly well known; its roots are not. Hooker chose the site because of its soil's characteristics—impermeable clay—and its sparse population. That was good planning at the time, but yesterday's rural chemical dump or airport often becomes tomorrow's suburb, as growth creeps outward. Customary practice in the 1940s was to pile up wastes in unlined surface impoundments in secure lagoons or pits—usually on the premises of a chemical factory—or to burn or dump wastes into rivers or lakes. Donald L. Baeder, Hooker's president and chief operating officer, told financial representatives in July 1980, that Love Canal was an appropriate waste disposal site, which had been used responsibly as landfill from 1942 until 1952. Even with all the advantages of hindsight, he points out, an American Institute of Chemical Engineers task force concluded that the original site design would essentially conform to most of federal regulations pending in the early 1980s.[2]

In 1952, when the land was no longer needed for disposal, Hooker deeded it to the Niagara Falls Board of Education, warning that chemical wastes made the area unsuitable for construction and including a contractual clause that absolved Hooker from any damages caused by the industrial waste. By accepting this deed, school disctrict counsel Ralph A. Boniello warned, the board was assuming liability for any possible damage.

The board proceeded. In 1954, it approved removal of up to 9,000 cubic yards of fill from the canal site, and the next year more. Despite Hooker's advice against subdivision, storm sewers were constructed across the landfill, cutting both the clay covering and the walls of the disposal area. Removals of soil continued; construction of homes began. Two concerns dominated the board minutes of the 1950s: construction of a new building and overcoming a monetary shortage. The long-term consequences of their actions did not appear to be considered. While developing the land, architect and contractor alike had to discover the chemical dump for themselves.

Baeder reacted to media and Board of Education accusations that Hooker had acted irresponsibly in its use and disposition of the canal. He pointed out that Hooker had not "foisted" the site upon an unsuspecting local school board, and had warned about previous use and the problems related to disturbing the protective cover. He cited correspondence with the school board, its minutes, articles from the local newspaper, and the deed. Hooker, before the transfer, made tests and inspections to determine that the clay walls had not permitted leaching of chemicals and that no drums containing chemicals were within four feet of the natural surface. A park would not have disturbed the site. Ironically, after all the passion and pain, that's what it will become. New York State has proposed a park after completion of remedial work.

What went wrong? Lots, according to Baeder. Chemicals migrated from the canal largely because the property was not maintained during the twenty-seven years after Hooker relinquished control. Intrusions—storm drains, sewer lines, and removal of fill—allowed surface waters to seep into the site. In 1976, after record precipitation, the canal overflowed like a bathtub, permitting chemicals to migrate onto adjoining properties. The remedial program to prevent further migration cost $2 million.

Those are the technical and legal aspects of a story that became a media event in August 1978, when a health emergency was declared. About twenty families with pregnant women and children younger than two were relocated from the first two rings of homes around the site. The evacuation was prompted by the suspected presence of chemicals in the basements of the homes, and fears of higher-than-expected levels of spontaneous abortions, miscarriages, and congenital malformations. The fear and anxiety that pervaded the population following this emergency declaration was the prime reason for the subsequent purchasing of the homes of 236 families and paying for their permanent relocation.

Media coverage created strong perceptions—many considered excessive today. First, concentrations of chemicals, measured by New York State and the EPA contractor, were lower than permitted under comparable government workplace standards, Hooker explains. Some of the chemicals singled out—chloroform, trichloroethylene, and tetrachloroethylene—either were not manufactured by Hooker while it used the canal for disposal or are considered ubiquitous.

Presence of chemicals was one concern; health was an important other. Here, too, Baeder notes that analysis of health data available from the New York Department of Health indicates that problems at Love Canal did not exceed those expected in the general population, and that no link was demonstrated between chemicals and health problems. But residents believed chemicals were present in dangerously high concentrations and health problems were rampant in their neighborhood. They responded very naturally and predictably with ever-increasing demands for permanent relocation. The government and the media frightened them, according to Hooker.

Love Canal may or may not have been polluted beyond repair by chemicals. Some media and cause-pushers decided it was. Eric Zuesse, in the February 1981 issue of *Reason*, blames the U.S. Justice Department; the EPA; various New York State agencies; Michael Brown, author of *Laying Waste*; and Lois Gibbs, president of the Love Canal Homeowners Association.[3] Why were they successful and Hooker's counterfight ineffective? According to Zuesse, Hooker wasn't helped by its parent, Occidental Petroleum Corporation, which met initial public relations challenges with a "practically unbroken string of catastrophically bad decisions." First, they tried stonewalling. Predictably, cracks appeared. Change was forced, but slowly. In 1980, Hooker publicly defended itself for the first time in a booklet, *Love Canal, The Facts*. Until then, the company had not boldly stated "We did not do it"; instead, as Zuesse puts it, it had given only "a meek squeak." The consequences were heavy: canal problems burned off $.5 billion of Occidental's stock value.

Nor did the company sue Brown or his publishers Random House for what Zuesse calls a libelous book. *Laying Waste* discusses toxic waste problems, not just in Niagara Falls, but throughout the country. A reporter, Brown talked with many residents, telling the story emotionally and mostly from their point of view. At first, Hooker met Brown's request for an interview with "prolonged silence," then agreed to some questions with Brown's publisher present. The journalist viewed this as an attempt to soften his reporting. Drums dumped in the canal, he writes, "contained a veritable witches' brew of chemistry, compounds of a truly remarkable toxicity. There were solvents that attacked the heart and liver." And he explains the dilemma of individuals and community—Hooker was vitally important as a provider of 3,000 blue-collar jobs and substantial tax revenues. Many feared distressing Hooker.

At first, Brown writes, ignorance and uncontrollable circumstances seemed responsible for the illnesses, not corporate insensitivity and ruthlessness. But it became apparent that the site was in fact "part of a general Hooker pattern." It dumped in other parts of town, too.[4]

In the public mind, even today, the company appears guilty. Yet anyone who digs into the matter must assess the temper and causes of the time, as expressed by government agencies, media, and issue-directed scientists. As Zuesse points out, Hooker may well have been the only participant that behaved responsibly. It chose an exceptionally fine chemical dump site; later, it ceded it to the school board under some threat of condemnation, but with warnings. Private winners may still become public punching bags, however.

In 1981, *The New York Times* editorialized: "When all the returns are in . . . it may well turn out that the public suffered less from the chemicals there than from the hysteria generated by flimsy research, irresponsibly handled."[5] Former New York Governor Hugh Carey commented: "The costly relocation of more than 700 homeowners . . . is medically unnecessary but has to be carried out to assuage the panic cause by the Environmental Protection Agency."[6] An article in *Science* concluded: the EPA may have hurt its suit against Hooker Chemical by causing panic at Love Canal, and also may have damaged its standing with the scientific community.[7]

What is happening today? In September 1985, *The New York Times* ran a headline: "Despite Toxic Waste, 350 Seek Love Canal Homes." "These days," the article read, "Love Canal, once home to 1,000 families has the air of a suburban ghost town. No children play, no dogs bark in the silent streets. In some less traveled sections, tufts of grass have started to sprout through cracks in the pavement. In front yards, overgrown shrubs have obscured the steps. Boards placed over broken windows have yellowed." Mayor Michael C. O'Laughlin, chair of the revitalization agency, is quoted: "Hysteria caused much of the problem. I don't feel the houses are in jeopardy at all." In August, two law suits were filed by a property owner and a businessman seeking a total of $15 million in damages from Occidental and Olin, the current owner of the 102nd Street dump.[8]

When an issue becomes inflamed and emotional, any company will take public lumps, fair or unfair. Attempting to calm the hysteria, speaking to genuine human concerns, showing a humane as well as business face, and telling the facts, loud and clear, frequently helps. While Hooker may have neglected this initially, the media and government agencies bear the brunt of the blame for "inherent dramatic hyperbole": Television reporters would say: "This is Love Canal. Here, below my feet, is what has been described as one of the worst . . . " In his review of Elizabeth Whelan's *Toxic Terror*, Daniel Henninger, assistant editorial page editor of the *Wall Street Journal*, wrote that the opinions of toxic terrorists lent credence to the most extreme interpretations of the health dangers posed by various chemicals and technologies whose value came under sustained attack. Journalists too often sought out horror-story scientists, while giving less or no space to authorities who would offer a more modest, qualified interpretation of events. This affiliation between environmentally extreme scientists and sensation-seeking media may be weakening. Henninger thinks toxic terrorists cried wolf too often. Journalists don't like getting burned by their sources—in this case, glib, all-purpose scientists.[9]

Love Canal, once a poignant example of Orwellian use of language, now illustrates that the two layers of the apparent and the real are merging into sober and instructive considerations for any company caught in the vise of an inflamed and not always accurately informed public.

## Even White Hats Get Hurt

Scandal haunts even companies long-known and respected for ethical operations and as good employers. GE, E.F. Hutton, and Union Carbide are current examples. Scandal surprises other companies, such as General Dynamics, who thought they were just doing what everyone else in the defense industry was, or what the government expected, only to find themselves singled out for censure.

During scandals, communications functions like medical triage on a battlefield: sorting out priorities under extreme pressure and shortages of time and resources. If communications and senior management ignore root causes, abuses metastasize, spreading the exposure. If managers permit too much public, unconvincing hype, credibility is lost. But, if used effectively—internally and externally—communications can help explain and mitigate damage. However, it cannot function as a mere blow-out patch creating false security and unconvincing images, and leaving managers to think that their job is done. Abuses must be cleaned up promptly, indictments answered. A public sense that nothing has changed or a second round of revelations court even greater disaster.

Trouble usually brews internally before it breaks into public awareness.

Curative procedures, logically, should start with analyzing operations and communication with employees. But communications must also address financial aspects: how to shore up the business and the stock price. Explain the extent of financial liability. Keep banks, vendors, and customers from unrealistic worry or desertion. Forestall a lynch mob mentality, which encourages lawyers, legislators, and media from attacking the wounded corporation.

Employees, dedicated for years, may be traumatized by wrong-doings exposed in headlines; embarrassed when friends question them about the scandal or when strangers ask where they work. Some years ago, when *Life* pictured a GE vice president in jail, employees were stunned; some wondered if they still wanted to work for GE. Many, fearing for their futures, may focus on personal concerns: writing and circulating resumes, networking rather than selling products. Even when Johnson & Johnson employees knew that their company was blameless and had been praised for its handling of the Tylenol recall, they still worried about their job security. Companies are brittle structures even in the best of times. When a company is guilty, it's worse. However, handled effectively, candidly, and promptly, the right messages can boost employees' morale mauled by a public scandal and redirect their thinking toward productivity and the future.[10]

Some employees may be angered and frustrated to see their company's once good name besmirched or singled out for legal action over practices accepted industry-wide. General Dynamics was accused for procedures that most defense contractors privately admit they normally followed. But conventions change. General Dynamics overstepped the bounds of the new propriety, and was made the example. How do companies react? Very differently, but usually poorly and seldom in their own best self-interests. Reacting quickly and candidly is the best damage control.

Repeatedly, however, companies initially attempt to stonewall, to fluff and puff internal messages. Some just plain lie. Others flirt with overexposure. Alan R. Bromberg, professor of law at Southern Methodist University, advised Texaco to tone down its public relations, fearing it could boomerang in Texaco's court proceedings against Pennzoil. Shouting disaster or threatening Chapter 11 could make Texaco creditors and suppliers very, very nervous, he explained.

Too much unconvincing *mea culpa* make the public wonder what manner of wimp is running things. Suddenly a chairman whom employees have seldom seen, much less heard, begins issuing soothing comments from every loudspeaker, appealing to workers from strategically placed video terminals.

(Even here, insensitivity shows. Often screens are placed in lunch areas, so workers feel that they cannot even eat without a message.) Letters—some sent home to families—memos, and advertisements attempt to convince employees and others over and over again that the company is decent and ethical, is being made a scapegoat or wrongfully accused.

Overkill is rampant. Previously unquestioned procedures are scrutinized minutely. Corporate cannons are rolled out to kill public gnats. The scape-goat search begins. Soapbox sermonizing sprouts. More letters, written like moralistic homilies, seek to dissuade the corporate flock from future sins. More systems, rigid checks and balances, are instituted. But the fallacy is relying on systems alone to do the job. Without a sense of individual ethical responsibility, employees bent on wrong-doing can still circumvent proce-dures in spirit and purpose. Review boards are created, and an ombudsman is appointed. Outside review by a court or government agency is accepted—although reluctantly. Words like ethics, integrity, reputation, and honesty are sprinkled throughout speeches, annual reports, shareholder letters, and interviews like raisins in a good coffeecake.

Adversity, however, can produce positive results. A thorough audit may reveal additional abuses that can be corrected before they damage publicly. Communicators like to say that such an exercise strengthens their hand for the next crisis. Maybe. After the initial shock and denial, employees may rally in defense of their employers; those previously tempted to wrong-doing may be dissuaded by seeing the penalties, formal and informal, meted out to wrong-doers. Every manager in one major company remembered vividly the psychological and corporate decline of a once-respected senior executive who was marched out of his suburban home at midnight in handcuffs in full view of his neighbors and family. He became a company ghost, present but neither seen nor acknowledged.

Does the public care about wrong-doing? Are they morally outraged, or forgiving? Or do they know or care only about the immediately relevant? Cynically, a company can profit from short memories. Ask a young execu-tive about the 1950s GE conviction for price fixing and he'll likely react with surprise.

Those intimately involved in companies under intense scrutiny tend to think everyone else is just as agonizingly aware, forever. Wrong. The author, immersed day by painful day in the details of accusations against Textron during the U.S. Senate confirmation hearings for its chairman G. William Miller to head the Federal Reserve System, shrank from talking to anyone. She wore obscuring fur hats and sunglasses in midwinter to keep from discussing details in the small Providence community. Chagrined, she realized few people knew much, fewer cared; relieved, she discovered that some supported the company, which had been a good neighbor to Providence for years.

E.F. Hutton's struggles illustrate the folly of rushing to resolve surface symptoms, in this case check kiting, while hoping to leave systemic causes intact. For more than a year Chairman Robert Fomon has tried, unsuccessfully, to remove Hutton "from the uncomfortable glare of public scrutiny and scandal."[11]

Executives in a fix similar to Fomon's can sympathize with his astonishment: "I never dreamed there would be an indictment." He explains that Hutton was caught in a political crossfire between Democrats out to embarrass the Republican-led Justice Department. A private, orderly man, "he is still groping to understand why he has been unable to contain the scandal," a profile in *The New York Times* concluded.[12]

Why is Hutton's chairman failing? First, he did not sufficiently take into account how unruly and uncontrollable the public turf is. Second, he thought one guilty plea alone would blunt public awareness of abuses. When that failed, he tried a single high-level investigation into practices by former Attorney General Griffith B. Bell. That failed to quell public outcries, too. Many people still think the executives involved escaped unscathed; many remain unconvinced they've seen the last of the abuses. Hutton is an industry leader. Who better to make an example of?

Third, white collar crimes are hot news. Legislators and courts sense that the public is tired of seeing the mighty apparently getting off easily. Paul Thayer, former business and Pentagon official, must have been shocked to be first convicted and jailed, then to be denied quick parole. Reading the temper of the times and news angles is vital. Fourth, and perhaps most important, internal actions lag behind demonstrated need. It took some time before Hutton's generally reported operational looseness was tightened; a smaller, more powerful board of mainly outside directors was organized; and different executives were put in charge. Robert Rittereiser, the new president, came from the outside, from a competitor, Merrill Lynch. Pleading guilty was the past; thorough housecleaning was still the future.

Cynical communicators think that the cleaner the company and the more respected it is for corporate responsibility and fine products, the greater is the desire either to mete out harsh judgments or dramatize every infraction. How much more satisfying to knock off the white hat, than to throw one more mudball at a black hat. General Electric is a case in point.

*Wall Street Journal* reporter Douglas R. Sease wrote that the company has long been regarded as one of the nation's exemplary corporations. But, along the way, it has also acquired a less enviable record. Three times in the past twenty-five years, GE has been convicted of price fixing, bribery and fraud. In April 1986, the company pleaded guilty to charges concerning missile warhead contracts.[13]

Although GE was not singled out alone, its "carefully burnished public persona made GE's crimes particularly jarring." Management's reaction suggested to Sease "how easily ethical standards can become blurred within big organizations." The incidents also showed how pressures can force otherwise honest people to violate their own principles and break the law. It becomes difficult for managers to enforce ethical standards, and to make sure the incidents are isolated, not encouraged by the system.

Lester Crown, long-time director of embattled General Dynamics, blames the system—the imperfect procurement system—for General Dynamic's troubles. He could have cited another: a senior management either unaware or unconcerned about over billings on defense contracts, then unable to staunch the criticism and publicity. Every executive should have a sign on his desk today: "There are no secrets."

A strong argument against wrong-doing—heeded more in hindsight than beforehand—is to imagine an action or memo in front page headlines or on the network news. Crown reflected, after the fact, on millions of dollars of improper overhead expenses—country club memberships, dog kennel fees, and personal use of corporate jets—all made to seem worse because a House committee discovered and announced that they had been charged against Pentagon contracts.[14]

The greatest trap is rationalizing actions and finding false safety in the assurance that peers in other companies share the same practices and perks. Given public sentiment, which thinks that corporate officers are too powerful and overpaid (although rock and sports stars who earn millions more escape the same censure), abuses—even when isolated—bait a skeptical public to call for harshly punishing the offenders. Any communicator worth his salt knows this, but he is pushing against the stream into personally perilous waters if he tries to bring this message to management. Often, he has little opportunity to prevent the abuse. Once it's in headlines, he may become the fall guy.

Executives suddenly find themselves embattled on unfamiliar terrain. To succeed, they must transform their mindset to understand how the "enemy" views the revelations. When General Dynamics Chairman and CEO David

S. Lewis faced a "barrage of bareknuckled questions from outraged legislators," all of his study of military strategy, all of his company's missiles, fighter planes, tanks, and submarines were useless.[15]

Few can control a troubled genie out of the bottle. But the predictable consequences usually surprise participants. The price is high. GD's troubles produced damaging publicity, greater government restrictions, Lewis' retirement, casualties within management ranks and financial accounts, loss of security clearances, damage to the defense industry, and diminished popular, even congressional, support for the defense budget. Investigations may become an Achilles' heel, damaging the industry and the nation's defense. "Being a defense contractor could be looked upon as having a license to steal."[16] A *Business Week*/Harris poll confirmed the public distrusts the defense establishment and thinks the game between contractors and government is rigged.[17]

These scandals and indictments have produced at least two long-range consequences crucial to communications. When legislators and activists are anxious to attack—in this case an incestuous military–industrial–congressional complex, academic could be added—it is stupid to think they will not find ammunition. Second, giving them a loaded gun is even dumber. Conversely, previous transgressions of defense contractors have been forgiven and forgotten once they disappear from the front page. That should militate against overreaction. However, even short-term damage, as Hutton and General Dynamics have experienced, can hurt extensively individuals, projects, and essential relations of trust. The challenge for the communicator is to convince the unscarred executive of those realities before the battle begins—and to keep his job.

## Flying Troubled Skies

More people died in air disasters during 1985 than ever before: victims of bombs, hijackings, wind shear, faulty design or maintenance, pilot misjudgment, or incomplete instructions from the ground. Cause, circumstance, location, and cultural response varied widely, but managing air disaster communications did not.

More diffuse and protracted crises—Tylenol, Bhopal, extensive scandals, and takeovers—require daily flexibility and long-term coping. While grace and intelligence under tension and media fire are just as important for airline crashes, the focus is more clearly defined: on people and just a few locations—the crash site and departure and arrival points. Thus, routine planning, lists of contacts and procedures are more important in airline disasters than in most other emergencies. This information should be on every manager's desk, not stashed away.[18]

Airline crashes happen without warning and are very visible: survivors and the media begin clamoring immediately for information. To cope, those experienced in handling crash communications offer these suggestions:

- Make available to the duty officer the names, phone numbers, and locations of all key airline officers, those who need to know in case of a crash, and members of federal and state agencies, such as the Federal Aviation Administration and the National Transportation Safety Board. Since accidents seem to happen perversely at the most inconvenient times—weekends, nights, and vacation times—standby phone numbers and alternates should be included.

- Establish functional priorities: who should be called in what order. It feeds any ego to call the CEO first, but lower-ranking managers may have a much greater need to know.

- Have statistics available on the type of plane, cruising speeds, number of seats, safety record, revenue, passenger miles flown without fatalities, names of the crew, and other details that help position the airline positively despite the accident. Such background furnishes balancing information to accompany pictures of burning wreckage and grieving survivors. (NASA officials were criticized for not having such statistics—the amount of liquid fuel in *Challenger*'s external tank—available for reporters after the explosion. The spokesman's lapse was compounded by turning the question away as if inappropriate.)

- Release crash information as soon as the facts and names can be verified and the next of kin notified. Here the interests of airlines and press coincide: to get as much information out as quickly as possible. Quick release expedites coverage, minimizes drawn-out follow-ups, and quells rumors, which are usually more horrible than the truth.

After one crash, for example, wild stories started circulating that a hospital had asked patients to sign release forms in return for money—victims were supposedly paid to sign away future claims. Actually, the airline had given patients small sums to tide them over; the forms merely acknowledged receipt of the money. Often stories circulate about spectral images walking away from burning wreckage, even after everyone has been accounted for.

The *Challenger* disaster also illustrates the problem of news lag. The agency ignored its own crisis plan, which calls for announcement of the crew's status within twenty minutes. It was made after five hours. Even after observers had witnessed the tragedy, reports came from a disembodied voice, not a flesh-and-blood NASA official. When an official did appear, the cosmetics were all wrong: Outdoors in poor lighting, which left faces totally in the dark or in deep shadows. Transmission was impaired by faulty sound connections. Nor did the representative say much that could not have been reported right after the explosion.

The success and apparent milk-run safety of space shuttles had gulled everyone, even NASA, into treating the launches as routine. *Challenger 10*'s explosion blasted a carefully created image of invincibility and of super-human technical and managerial proficiency. It also caught the space agency's leadership in disarray and public information people ill-prepared. William Safire noted in a column in *The New York Times*, "Handling Bad News," the space agency's leadership was in flux—the director, indicted for fraud, had been forced into a leave of absence; his successor had been in place just one week when the accident happened. The former public information officer had just been replaced.

And, NASA missed the chance to put human feeling into their announcements. Although President Reagan sensitively spoke to school children, who had been attracted by all the prelaunch hoopla and the media's almost exclusive focus on the presence of an all-American school teacher, NASA ignored the students. They misused their own public relations theme. Safire concludes that NASA showed a shadowy and ill-prepared face to the world. Its reputation for sophisticated and effective public relations had taught everyone to expect better.

A no-no from every point of view—legal, insurance, and other liabilities—is speculating on the causes of a crash. One communicator bridled when the legal department, worried about disclosure, advised the company to say nothing, do nothing, admit nothing. Some middle ground must be brokered. Causes are appropriately announced by the National Transportation Safety Board only after thorough investigation. Usually there are several interlocking causes; the truth may be hidden by the immediately apparent. The Japanese wisely distinguish between *honne*, truth, and *tatemae*, appearance.

Hijacking or attempted extortion is more complicated to handle than a crash. In such cases, the airline's obligation is totally to the passengers and their security, not to the press. Terrorists listen to press reports and bask in the attention. One way of balancing the hype is by providing background on earlier hijackings—how they were handled, how passengers fared. For instance, Cuba, once the destination for many hijackers, usually returned most passengers quickly and safely.

Despite all their highly visible, emotional troubles, airlines are more fortunate than many other companies. The Food and Drug Administration requires pharmaceutical companies to run corrective ads for false claims, and to announce widely and expensively any product dangers or withdrawals from the market. Newspapers routinely list restaurants that violate health and safety codes. Such punishments or shame ads are not required of other corporations whose employees also make life-and-death decisions. U.S. airlines with documented deficiencies do not have to express remorse or give a public apology. Rather, some officials are prone to speak of disappointment not with their company's workers, but with the FAA for imposing fines: nuisance regulators at work again.

Questions of public shame illustrate cultural differences in air crashes.[19] When the Japanese airline, JAL, suffered its worst-ever crash in August 1985—520 dead—the airline followed an elaborate protocol to atone: personal apologies by the company's president, memorial services, and financial reparations. For weeks, more than 400 airline employees helped bereaved relatives with everything from arranging funeral services to filling out insurance forms. All advertising was suspended voluntarily. Had JAL not made these acts of conciliation, it would have courted charges of inhumanity and irresponsibility.

At the memorial service, JAL's president, Yasumoto Takagi, bowed low and long to relatives of the victims, bowed again to a wall covered with wooden tablets bearing the victims' names. He asked forgiveness and accepted responsibility. This uniquely Japanese sensibility did not, however, stem persistent criticism from politicians and the media, nor did it cushion the company from the realities of a business downturn. The crash also brought about dramatic changes. The president and several other senior managers resigned or retired; the maintenance chief committed suicide. And the future became much more competitive as domestic customer demand slumped and other airlines competed on international routes. It is difficult to see how JAL can transform this misfortune into a benefit, as an old Japanese saying advises.

Airlines' crisis planning must center on people: a possible media advantage. With the press penchant for human interest stories, crash communications can be somewhat easier and more straightforward than those involving other industrial emergencies. A major explosion at a chemical plant or mine is complicated: the scene might be dangerous, chemical formulas may not be easily understood, or their affect on the public may not be fully known. But woe to the profit and loss sheet of any airline that comes across as unfeeling, that lies, or that continues to be weakened publicly by other crashes or near misses.

---

## Looking Beyond the Bottom Line: Expensive Product Disasters

When crucial questions of product quality and safety are stifled by internal politics, absence of corporate courage, or a focus purely on profits—what the product will reap in the market rather than what it may cost in the courts—expensive troubles are brewing. Too often ignored is what withdrawal of public trust will cost not just the product under fire, but all the company makes.

There's nothing new about the fact whistleblowers are few, usually pilloried, and almost universally ignored as nags or cause-pushers. In the last century, Henrik Ibsen in *Enemy of the People* dramatized the unworthiness of those who do not dare. He understood that truth is in the minority—the first casualty in corporate wars.

Examples of obtuseness abound, from basic quality control to disasters such as the Dalkon Shield. In one food company, pseudo scientific tasting designed to test product merit alone was debased into questions of who was the brand manager. Rating tended to be based on his political stature and power. As a result, some ill-tasting flops went to market, some good products died in the testing stalls. Although this cost the company some product leadership and market share, it did not court the disaster that silence and cover-ups have brought upon some pharmaceutical companies.

To cite several current examples: Monsanto bought threats of hundreds of suits when it acquired G.D. Searle & Co., maker of the Copper 7, an intra-uterine device. Eli Lilly and Company pleaded guilty to criminal charges that it failed to inform the federal government about four deaths and six illnesses related to its arthritis drug, Oraflex. Although few pharmaceutical companies have ever faced criminal charges, Smithkline Beckman pleaded guilty to such charges for failing to report the lethal side effects of its blood pressure drug, Selacryn.

The most tragic illustration of a good company making a greedy mistake and trying to smother effective communications is A.H. Robins, producer of the Dalkon Shield. The company enjoyed great respect and financial strength. These cherished attributes may have blinded it to the need for scrupulous self-examination and to an understanding of how quickly a good name can be tarnished.

In 1970, Robins bought rights to an allegedly superior IUD called the Dalkon Shield. This single decision, compounded by subsequent cover-ups, destruction of evidence, and tasteless inquiries into the personal hygiene and sexual practices of litigates, plunged Robins into a descending spiral. In August 1985, it filed for preemptive bankruptcy.

At first, the company ignored early warnings of serious health risks; later, it chose to conceal them. It suppressed or misinterpreted physician and employee complaints; it ignored independent medical studies that questioned the birth control device's safety and reliability. When lawsuits started, documents were either destroyed or withheld on improper claims of privilege. Little thought apparently was given to how the public would react.

As in most visible crises, lapse was laid upon lapse. Robins was not the sole irresponsible player. Few others spoke out initially, even though one health organization estimated that as many as 500,000 wearers might have been injured by the shield. Nor did the federal government take quick and effective remedial steps. The FDA waited four years after the first reports of trouble to investigate the shield and then, after the product was removed from the market, did little to ensure the device was removed from women still wearing it. Lawyers, eager for a quick dollar, advertised for shield clients, gave them assembly line treatment, and settled as quickly as possible for whatever they could get. One book on the subject, *Nightmare,* views this as a story of corporate greed, blind consumer trust, government ineffectiveness, and medical apathy.[20]

Robins' actions set it on a path of public deceit from which its reputation probably will never recover. Some observers equate the legal and moral cover-up to Watergate. As of mid-1985, at least 21 women were dead, at least 13,000 were sterile or infertile, and probably hundreds more were mothers of damaged children. And 16,000 liability cases are logjammed in the courts.

Some critics say that the tragedy was created because Robins officials looked only at the bottom line, ignoring the long-term impacts. Gross revenues from sale of the shield were about $11 million, which pales beside the company's worth and the millions in claims it risked and lost. As of June 30, 1985, Robins had paid $375 million in damages, $25 million in punitive damages, and $107 million in legal expenses. And those figures do not include loss of the customer confidence vital to the pharmaceutical industry. Robins traded off visible potential profits and invisible liabilities. Losses from drugs not sold do not show on the balance sheet or make great copy.

The shield decisions also demonstrate the chasm between the flesh-and-blood person and the paper corporation executive. Face-to-face, an individual may be charitable, civic-minded, and caring. Behind the corporate veil, the same individual—forgetting or lacking the imagination to understand the impact of his own actions or what he is asking others to do—can wound and kill. It's like the desk-bound, bureaucratic military commander who does not fully understand the pain and death he is ordering the grunts into.

Judge Miles Lord, in his stern and unusual lecture from the bench of corporate executives, called the Robins case an accumulation of corporate wrongs that manifest individual sin. He admonished company executives to lift their eyes from that guiding beacon, the bottom line. Actually, if they had weighed all the components of the bottom line—not just profit from sales—they would have made much more profitable decisions. The consumer movement of the 1960s called it "above the bottom line."

After all the costly public disasters, many managers still neglect to factor possible public liabilities into their product and other planning. Even a wise business decision can turn financially sour if not handled well publicly. A poor decision, compounded by attempts to hide or stonewall once the press focuses in on product problems and consumer complaints, is a prescription for serious, long-term trouble.

## The Greatest Tragedy: Bhopal

Few industrial tragedies have been as grave, complicated, or covered as widely as the December 4, 1984, leak of 40,000 kilos of methylisocyanate gas into the atmosphere around a pesticide plant operated in Bhopal by the Indian subsidiary of Union Carbide Corporation. Horror resulted: approximately 1,700 dead, thousands injured, and many thousands more condemned to suffer aftereffects throughout their lives.

The tragedy raised management questions that will fuel business school debates for years. Did careless supervision, faulty equipment, sabotage, or all of the above cause the initial water leak? How responsible was the American parent? The Indian subsidiary? Where were the major decisions on design, maintenance, and managers made or cleared? In India? At corporate head-quarters? Where is the legal venue? How damaging to the United States and the legal profession was the spectacle of death-chasing lawyers rushing to Bhopal? Should squatters be permitted to live—or return—near plants pur-posely built in remote areas? What misunderstandings and faulty assump-tions were bred by cultural differences? By nationalism vis-à-vis a multi-national?

Carbide is paying very dearly in all ways. Perhaps terminally. When the tragedy hit, the company was just beginning to shed its reputation as a pol-luter. CEO Warren Anderson was widely respected as a good, decent, and caring executive. Long-range strategy focused on Carbide's strong and well-known consumer products. One leak changed everything.

The communications implications of Bhopal will haunt not just Carbide, but other companies and CEOs for a long, long time. The questions cut to the very core of executive visibility, media and community relations, absent press experts, and unforeseen disaster—life-threatening to people and corpo-ration.

First, should Anderson have gone to India? Probably not. He made his decision immediately, explaining, "I sort of felt that if I were over there I could make judgments and decisions on the spot."[21] He was spurred by humanitarian concerns to speed aid to all who needed it. But this humane, responsible, even generous gesture accomplished little. Anderson was jailed briefly, denied access to the plant, and threatened with criminal proceedings. On the first anniversary, he was burned in effigy. Despite all of his good intentions, human feeling seemed to be lacking in the company's responses. And his presence encouraged a focus on one individual as responsible.

In retrospect, Anderson should have sent his chief operating officer, more medical assistance, trained media people, and possibly even encouraged the trade press to go. They could have reported knowledgeably on complicated questions of chemical production and safeguards.

Like many of his peers, before Bhopal the chief executive was very private and kept a low profile. Suddenly he was thrust into the grueling public spot-light, forced to balance often conflicting demands of stockholders, company attorneys, reporters, employees, congressmen, foreign governments, and other constituencies. If you listen to lawyers, he told a reporter from *The New York Times*, you would lock yourself up in a room somewhere; if you listen to your public relations people, you would answer everything and appear on every television program. These dilemmas are familiar to communicators faced with lawyers who want to say nothing, but who know that information vacuums are always filled—usually to the company's detriment. Experienced communicators use the CEO's presence very judiciously: only in the forum and time most appropriate and useful. Reporters naturally seek to talk as high up in a company as they can. Once Anderson's trip made him the Carbide symbol, it was more difficult for others to act as spokesmen. Practically, Bhopal meant that Anderson had to turn over to others responsibility for day-to-day operations.

Carbide has been criticized rather widely for its media relations during the Bhopal tragedy—somewhat unfairly considering the distances, language-barrier, magnitude of the crisis, and the general lack of information. Anderson himself relates his frustration at getting news first from television. Other contacts were difficult or slow. Some perceived the company as unresponsive, confused, inept, reluctant, or unable to provide information. At best, confusion reigned initially; at worst, media relations were botched. It is difficult to make a fair judgment, even now. Some communicators criticized the company's initially cautious, defensive stance; it neither admitted knowledge of the cause nor accepted blame. Some interpreted stonewalling the press as concern about legal liability and suits.

"No comment," always a red flag to the bullpen of reporters, produced several negative articles. "No comment" may have been the only possible answer, but other words should have been used. Today, pleading the Fifth Amendment implies guilt. In like manner, "no comment" means that you have something to hide, not that information simply is not available or not yet verified.

Despite enormous public interest, no press relations specialist went to India—very typical, even in a communications crisis. Most communicators are treated as ancillary, called in after the major decisions are made, when it is too late to take simple corrective actions to prevent major public damage to the company. Or they are shunted aside when something very visible or exciting is happening, even in the communications area. Every executive is his own PR man until he's in deep trouble, and sometimes even then. Nor was the press assisted well in the aftermath of the Bhopal tragedy. Stuart Diamond of *The New York Times* was denied official access to workers and exworkers, officials and others, both in the United States and in India. Naturally, he found other sources.

Coverage, though extensive, omitted some Indian realities. The press quickly alleged gross negligence at the plant, primitive safety precautions, workers not wearing required safety equipment, understaffing of the plant, and unavailability of critical spare parts. The press was not equally as hard on the lawyers who rushed in, or on India. Author Ved Mehta, an Indian, detailed how the health, living, and commuting conditions of local workers could have made the Bhopal plant more accident-prone. Another journalist criticized the "notorious Indian bureaucracy's" irregular and insensitive handling of unfortunate survivors. Hundreds of the dead were cremated without being taken to hospitals, which means no death certificate and possibly no financial aid to the surviving family. Bribes were sought. Victims became entangled in disputes over who was responsible for what and in red-tape-bound relief efforts.

Carbide, while concentrating on the Bhopal tragedy, made another classic communications management mistake. When an industry or company is under intense scrutiny, when it is hot, every operation must be squeaky clean. Assumptions and assurances are not enough; Cussed, I'm-from-Missouri checks must be made. Any sister plant, particularly in another developing nation, must be as safe as possible. After another leak from a Carbide plant, headlines read:

"West Virginia Officials Assailing Delay in Alert"

"250 Flee Toxic Cloud as Train Derails in Arizona"

"A Toxic Chemical Spill in Camden; 35 Injured and 200 Evacuated After Dye Plant Accident—3,000 Gallons Leak"

"Spill of Caustic Agent Routs Hundreds Near Washington"[22]

In August 1985, a leak of a toxic gas, aldicarb oxime, from Carbide's plant in Institute, West Virginia, sent 135 people to the hospital and the company's credibility plunging still further. Once more the communications and management doors was closed. Prompt reporting of leaks was promised, again. Even after Bhopal, many West Virginians still regarded Carbide as a major employer and a good corporate citizen. They accepted its assurances that warnings would be given in sufficient time for safe evacuation. Now they wondered and worried. Back-to-back incidents eroded the long-standing confidence of employees and supporters of the chemical industry; many began to question the safety of chemical facilities in the Kanawha Valley.

Now the company could talk itself blue in the face and people would remain skeptical. Or, as Anderson put it, "If we have a release of Arpege [at the plant] 135 would go to the hospital." The second accident at Institute weakened the negotiating position with India. Coming on the heels of Bhopal, Institute became a turning point in concern. It made the unthinkable thinkable—again.

Then came the watermelon scare. Temik, a highly effective but controversial insect killer manufactured by Carbide is based on the same toxic chemical that escaped from Bhopal. Even though federal authorities had barred Temik from use on watermelon crops (unlike other fruits, watermelons retain the pesticide), it was misapplied by some farmers seeking to save money. Temik kills bugs with only one application, unlike other pesticides, which require several. The sickness caused by Temik has flu-like symptoms, but is not life-threatening. Nonetheless, Carbide was back in credibility-damaging headlines. Carbide's association made farmers and consumers fear and claim the worst.

As a result of Carbide's problems and those of other chemical companies, Americans are beginning to demand a right to know more of potential hazards. Although chemical companies have opposed greater disclosure in the past, arguing that trade secrets would be involved, they are accepting the necessity, given current suspicions. Monsanto Company is distributing information about possible hazards and precautions to residents near its fifty plants. The Chemical Manufacturers Association is preparing guidelines for its members. It also is considering a national clearinghouse for information about toxic chemicals, and exploring ways to develop better emergency response plans in cooperation with local citizens.[23] Other companies are attempting to allay the fears of their neighbors by inviting them to open houses, to see the production and safety precautions that go on behind the fences. In India, Bhopal quite simply has changed everyone's consciousness about what companies must do to make operations safe.

Bhopal's impact on Carbide and its management is staggering. Aside from the direct tragedy-related problems of litigation and public relations, the depressed stock price and need to conserve cash to cover legal claims against the company, halted its aggressive acquisition policy. Write-offs and charges resulted in a $371 million loss for the first three quarters of 1985, compared with earnings of $310 million for the same nine months of 1984.

To fend off successfully a late-1985 tender offer by Samuel J. Heyman, CEO of GAF, Carbide decided to sell the consumer products line upon which it had planned to build its future. More than 4,000 employees were terminated. Acres of headquarters property in Connecticut were put up for sale. A comprehensive—some say long overdue—restructuring was undertaken. A smaller Carbide may still be viable, but with consumer products gone, it is in exactly the position its long-range strategy was attempting to avoid: dependence on less stable, cyclical, mature businesses.

Anderson, long known for his sensitivity to employee concerns, for his chats with them over breakfast in the company cafeteria, has made morale-boosting videotapes for employees worldwide. Some report employee morale was high after Bhopal. Many worked harder and contributed $150,000 to relief efforts. Restructuring and layoffs, however, have left many bitter. They thought, unwisely, that Carbide would take care of them for life.

How could the company have handled its communications differently?

- First, involve communicators when major decisions are being made, and treat their counsel not as nay-saying or do-goodism, but as wise cautionary advice.

- Second, imagine worst-possible scenarios, ultimate disasters, then prepare as much as any individual or company can for handling them.

- Third, initially be more candid with the press. Who understands better the difficulties of gathering accurate information on a fast-breaking major story at great distance, during an engulfing emergency?

- Fourth, with all the clarity of 20/20 hindsight, run operations to minimize emergencies and to be sensitive to surrounding conditions and national practices. Ask how a safety lapse would look on the front page or the network news. Months after the accident, Anderson reported conditions were so poor, so unprofitable, at the Bhopal plant in December, it should not have been operating.

Despite all, in a letter to shareholders, the chief executive pointed to clear signs of progress. But a news report may be closer to the mark. It noted Carbide had fallen deeper into a corporate quagmire: litigation, overburdened management, and public cynicism about safety. And the problems appeared to be growing worse. Carbide successfully fended off GAF, but was left highly leveraged; dependent on cyclical, limited growth businesses; and with a sullied public image.

Soon Carbide was back in damaging headlines. In April 1986, the Occupational Safety and Health Administration proposed a $1.4 million fine—the largest penalty in its history—for 221 alleged health and safety violations at Carbide's Institute plant. Labor Secretary William Brock lashed out at what he termed "complacency" and "willful disregard for health and safety." The company termed these charges "grossly distorted" and vowed to appeal the proposed fines.[24]

At the risk of redundancy, the communications lessons of Bhopal are clear: Once a company or industry is the cynosure of public attention, only scrupulous examination of every operation and action is sufficient. Every weakness potentially damaging or expensive must be cleaned up, corrected, or explained—convincingly. That, ultimately, is the only way to protect a company's public reputation and its bottom line.

# 7

# Winning with Communications

A NY corporate activity shares successes and failures with others, but communications, by its very nature, must be both more deeply and more widely involved in the organization. Few communicators enjoy the satisfaction of their lawyer peers, who can point to winning an important decision, or of a product manager, who can dramatize the ascent of sales. And much that communications does is unglamorous or soon-forgotten damage control.

But sometimes communications can quell rumors, potentially damaging to business; can demonstrate how dramatic graphic and verbal public presentations can distinguish a company; or can plan long-range with marketing to create a craze for a product. During the past decade, managements have been forced to reverse optimistic, expansive business plans: rather than open new markets, they must close or shrink unprofitable ones; must terminate rather than recruit employees. When the community unit is small, the operation vested with emotion, and the workforce into its second or third generation of dedication, the challenges are particularly acute. In all the examples discussed in this chapter, communications became the catalyst for solving a corporate or marketing problem.

## Banking Against Rumors

Rumors damage any business, but few more than banking, which is grounded on the implicit trust of its customers. The mere whiff of trouble— even when denied cogently, convincingly, and quickly—can start a run on deposits. When savings are endangered, something in our shared psyches flashes danger, panic. Usually objective business ears open to hearsay. The media delight in showing long lines of people waiting overnight for banks to open—the worse the weather conditions, the deeper the scare, the better the story. Lines become infectious and impel many other patrons to get their money out fast. Millions of dollars can be lost on a single shred of misinformation.

What can be done, short of slamming shut bank doors until realism has replaced rumors? One answer, very simple in conception but seldom practiced, is to conduct business honestly with an eye to public exposure. Unfortunately, after-the-fact denials and attempted cover-ups are more common. Bank of Boston's public relations horror show, the cozy naive relations between Ohio regulators and bankers that contributed to the Home State Savings Association going bust, Bank of America's highly visible actions, as well as the American Banking Association's preventive work, document the range of financial communications problems.

Bank of Boston hid from the media until serious allegations surfaced. Then bank executives came out slugging like tough guys. Two wrongs made the situation worse. Chairman William L. Brown held his first press conference in his thirty-six years with the bank to deny reported links between the bank and organized crime. The bank tried to characterize currency reporting problems as a systems error. These efforts revealed just the tip of serious communications problems that had been building for years.[1]

The bank operated very privately and aloofly. It projected an elitist, uncaring attitude and suffered from a reputation for heavy-handedness. Consequently, it became a voodoo doll, easily stuck with pins by community organizers and Boston politicians who were eager to blame local economic woes on unfeeling bankers.

Instead of confessing to lapses promptly, Chairman Brown took on the media in a letter to shareholders. He complained of "inaccuracies and misunderstandings," but never mentioned on-going investigations. Communications dinosaurs believe they can dish out anything when in trouble: the public will believe it. The public reads nothing else. Wrong, as Bank of Boston discovered when it tried to deny that its international dealings had come under scrutiny.[2]

The quagmire of public communications seems beguilingly easy beforehand. Its harshness and tenacity only appear when it is too late to recoup. Internal wishfulness dominates; ramifications are minimized or deemed easy to control. Executives assume secrets can be kept, the rowdy public controlled, and business conducted as usual. Bank of Boston fell into all these traps and is now reaping a harvest of ill will: closed accounts, federal investigations, and expected state hearings into its international activities. Doubtless, the management was stunned. But the worst mistakes lay not in stonewalling, nor in acting only when under censure; rather they were made in not factoring the public response into initial decisions, then trying to tough it out.

Cincinnati-based Home State suffered from internal casualness and unfounded assumptions concerning regulators, which resulted in massive failure to regulate the savings and loan. A whistleblower is never popular; in this case, superiors simply ignored him. He was not surprised when the association went bust early in 1985. It seemed as if the trivial stymied the important. A pencil draft wouldn't do; his report must be typed. When it was, some mentions of a cease and desist order were deleted. Regulators relied on assurances grandly given, on productive ties between savings and loan superintendents and Home States' chairman, Marvin Warner. They wasted time and effort fighting over who was autonomous and who subordinate. The saga is over.[3] Its communications message is simple: abuses only fester when swept under carpets by influence, wishful thinking, assurances based on quicksand, or lack of institutional courage. Once abuses are public—and they are guaranteed to be—it's only worse.

When a company is big and visible in an industry under intense scrutiny, crisis becomes the everyday norm—no longer an isolated spike on a communications fever chart. The bigger the institution, the longer the needles and the more needles. That's exactly the situation Ronald E. Rhody stepped into when he became senior vice president of Bank of America. We're too big to hide, too important to be ignored, Rhody told the San Francisco Public Relations Roundtable. Measured by deposits and depositors, B of A is the largest bank in California and the United States. In absolute terms, it is the biggest earner in the state and fifth in the country.[4]

"No other industry has been caught up in a maelstrom of such massive change," Rhody noted, "confronted with such stress and strain, cast in such a malevolent economic and political environment, or scrutinized so intensively and extensively by media and government in such a compressed time frame" as banking. National uneasiness about banks generally is heightened by well-publicized worries about repayment of loans to developing countries and failures of financial institutions.

Understandably, B of A became the litmus test for the industry. Its own actions attracted even more attention. In 1984, the bank closed more branches than most others have. Even so, its branch network is still the country's largest. As a result of this and other actions, Rhody reported that, between September 1984 and May 1985, the bank was "favored" with twenty-six major negative news breaks or situations with negative potential, which drew extensive attention in almost every major publication and wire service. To cope, Rhody and his staff developed strategies and wisdoms of value not only to banking, but to other industries under public pressure.

First, two schools of press relations exist, crisis or no. The take-charge school gives a corporation the best chance of getting the story told right. The company tells it first: defines the problem, sets the context, and, in some instances, preempts criticism. The other, the sit-on-it school, according to Rhody, is arrogant and only delays the day of reckoning. It also flies in the face of reality: there are no secrets anymore.

Second, it is vital to level with the media, or they will just go elsewhere to seek information. Granted, the media can surprise with unanticipated questions, or all the facts may simply not be known yet. Legal, competitive, or negotiating positions could be damaged by premature or incomplete release of information. Internal clearances, although quickly criticized by an impatient press, are essential for the communications officer. He needs the cooperation of peers to get information. Surprise peers with a press announcement, exclude them from the clearance loop, and he's in trouble. Conversely, the corporate spokesperson should not allow himself to be forced into releasing information just because an editor says he is going to write a story anyway.

In dealing with specific situations, the B of A's management aimed to:

- Limit liability.

- Cushion the investors involved.

- Determine whether similar exposure existed elsewhere in the bank and impose strict safeguards to prevent further incursions.

- Protect the privacy of employees being investigated.

- Maximize possibilities of recovery.

Communicators implemented this strategy by:

- Telling shareholders as quickly and accurately as possible the extent of the loss.

- Maximizing opportunities for recovery by not exposing investors whom speculating publicity might damage.

- Protecting the privacy of discussions so that settlements with investors could be reached sans the glare of public attention.

What did Rhody and the Bank of America learn from these experiences? First and foremost: candor is the best policy. Admitting that you don't know or are not going to answer a particular question is not as damaging as attempting to cover up or lie.

A negative story is not the end of the world. Others have been there and survived. Some people won't see it. Others will view it skeptically, as more a matter of media hype than substance. Still others will understand it for the blip it may in truth be. Thick skins and objectivity in media relations should be as required as MBAs are elsewhere in a corporation.

Rhody concludes that planning has no substitute: he who wings it is a dummy. But a plan is merely a road map, not the journey. It will not succeed if treated as a rigid be-all-end-all.[5]

Rumors — "improvised news" — plague financial institutions generally. Frederick Koenig, professor of sociology at Tulane University, points out that the trader's jungle drums are among the most sensitive in the world.[6] Rumor has as strong an influence as fact on the prices of commodities and companies. Pennzoil Company stock soared in January 1986 on rumors that it had received an attractive tax-free takeover offer from its legal sparring partner, Texaco. Proclivity to rumor is endemic to a business where everyone operates with high-powered antenna. People under stress need order and a feeling of completion, need to assemble pieces so they make sense. Hard facts and verification cannot always keep pace with hearsay. Koenig illustrates his points with Continental Illinois, which was done in by rumors, and Manufacturers Hanover, which survived. Granted, Manny Hanny's situation was more easily and factually explained.

No secret, Continental was in trouble. It bought $2 billion in loans that became worthless when Penn Square Bank in Oklahoma went bust. Continental's $3 to $4 billion in loans to Third World countries might not be repaid. Within the bank and in the market people grew jittery. A great seedbed for hearsay.

Bits and pieces of rumor that Continental was on the verge of bankruptcy or filing for Chapter 11 (banks can do neither) began circulating among people with limited knowledge of banking and finance. The very outlandishness of the stories lulled bankers into a false sense of security. The bank's treasurer denied "the preposterous rumors." Instead of quelling the incorrect, he merely focused more attention on the bank's difficulties.

Panic followed rumor. A Japanese journalist gave substance to speculations by reporting that a New York bank had "disclosed" the possible purchase of Continental by a Japanese financial institution. Wide coverage of this "news" widened the panic. It stopped only when the federal government threw its full faith and credit behind Continental in an unprecedented attempt to halt an international run on the bank and prevent a wider crisis.

Even so, a general uneasiness and lack of confidence continues to infect financial institutions. Manufacturers Hanover was hit next. Word circulated in May 1984 that the bank could not fund itself because of a 3⅜-point drop in its stock price, heavy exposure to Latin American borrowers, and its liquidation of its portfolio of British government bonds.

Manny Hanny had an easier time than the Illinois Bank in staunching rumors. The bank had posted high earnings the previous year—the twelfth consecutive year. And the rumor, itself a sign of troubled, uncertain times, was very specific, hence easier to refute. The positive reaction was swift, partly because enough people with sufficient background could judge the realities of the situation.

To counter rumors, Professor Koenig first counsels credibility. Denials from a captain that his ship is not sinking will hardly be believed when water is obviously pouring into staterooms. Second, business could adopt to its benefit the practice of many cities, which have set up rumor-control centers to deal with natural disasters. But, Koenig concludes, rumors in the financial world will probably continue, perhaps become even more prevalent. As computers and electronic communications continue to speed information, bombarding people without giving them the time or wisdom to understand and evaluate the material, stress and anxiety will grow. People will conjecture and talk. An old World War II poster warned a careless slip of the lip would sink a ship. Careless talk, the more amorphous the more dangerous, can likewise damage banking.

The American Banking Association assists financial institutions in preparing before they get into public difficulties and in speaking out in their self-interest.[7] State associations are encouraged to participate in media training seminars to help them handle incidents such as bank robberies or a crisis in confidence. Scare stories are rare, but very damaging when they occur. The ABA suggests taking the sting out of situations by educating the public beforehand. The surprise can be taken out of nonperforming loans, for example, by explaining the market discipline regulators impose to insure that these loans perform in a safe and sound manner. Specific techniques are suggested also. When a newspaper ran misinformation about a bank, it not only responded to that publication, but conducted a wide-ranging information campaign including all the media and coffee klatsches with bank officials. This broke the web of fabrication.

The ABA is focusing currently on three legislative areas: basic banking, rate disclosure, and uncollected funds. Banks are urged to participate through materials designed to brief members on the current consumerists' positions and perceptions, outlines of federal and state legislative activity, practical guidelines for implementation strategies, and samples of materials to spread the local banks' positive message.

Banking is more in the limelight and under more intense scrutiny than ever before. This calls for greater public relations expertise from banks and a significantly better-trained breed of journalists covering banking.

## The Devil and P&G

Moving quickly to squash stories—even one as ridiculous as the rumor that Procter & Gamble's products were promoting the devil's work—is the only way to go. Otherwise, rumors evolve, emerge, and go underground, only to reemerge and recycle, each time with greater force, outlandishness, and potential damage. Quick, authoritative denial, substantiated by as many facts as possible—even if the most fervent rumor-mongers ignore them— limits the damage.

The dynamics of the devil story paralleled an earlier tale that McDonald's was putting worms into its hamburgers and that its executives had discussed the rumors on the Donahue television show. Neither story was true, but reality did not stay the rumors. The companies reacted differently. McDonald's refuted the stories immediately; P&G acted more slowly.

Rumors of the giant consumer products company's connection to the Church of the Devil had been circulating for about three years. Initially, the devil story and an associated tale that P&G's man-in-the-moon logo was the sign of the devil were more of an annoyance than a threat to sales. But news coverage spread. Housewives began clearing their kitchens of the "devil's products" and demanding that supermarkets do the same. One Cleveland television commentator, Dick Feagler, wondered if he should throw out all his detergents and toothpaste, or engage an exorcist to banish the devil. He complained that, "Instead of ignoring the yahoo, red-necked, hair-brained gaggle of self-raptured morons that started this drool, [P&G] has bowed to their sensitivities." Easily said, when you are not watching sales decline and reading damaging headlines.

Although P&G executives knew the stories were ridiculous, they became an "enormous distraction." The company spent probably several hundred thousand dollars on antirumor public relations, extra phone staff, detectives to track rumors to their source, and four lawsuits filed against people said to be rumor-mongers.

Eventually, P&G gave the devil his due, dropping the symbol from future package designs, while retaining it on company letterheads, the annual report, and the Cincinnati headquarters building. Executives explained that the 103-year-old man in the moon no longer had any real promotional value. It was easier to expunge it.

These actions stopped further publicity and spread of rumors. Daily call counts about Satan dropped from as many as 500 to 50, and 15 percent of those supported P&G's actions.[8]

A rumor, crazy and irrational as it is to executives, cannot be dismissed out of hand until its sources and seedbed are analyzed. If people want to believe the craziest untruth and act upon it, any company can be damaged.

---

## Federal Express: Marsupial Marketing

Rather than hand-wringing over diminished market opportunities, innovators look harder for the niche, the marsupial pouch, in which to grow a new business. It must not only supply a need—in the case of Federal Express, overnight delivery of small packages—but must communicate its services vividly, in refreshing, pungent language that speaks to today.

Fred Smith, founder of the highly successful Federal Express, sought such a niche. By adapting a wartime technique—hubbing flights—he created a company almost single-handedly.

Despite astonishingly rapid changes in operating habits and marketing, American business clings, as if to a security blanket, to the antiquated medium of paper. Authority is vested in paper. The same piece is passed from hand to hand—even across country.

Based primarily on his Vietnam experience, Smith determined that the speedy delivery of small packages was a potentially profitable niche. Existing services moved packages like passengers: comfortably, directly, but slowly. Smith realized that fast, on-time delivery was the key. Senders did not care about the route their package took to its destination, just when it arrived. What would be unacceptable inconvenience and routing to an air passenger was dispatch for a package. Smith's concept of hubbing—now being adapted by passenger airlines—and much of his initial planning demonstrate involved marketing savvy. Implementation was a tour de force in communicating in vivid, effective language and graphics.

The company's image was carefully planned and nurtured. Considerable time and money was spent to position Federal Express as a progressive, opportunistic, efficient company—to Smith, the prototype of a new generation of ventures to be spawned late in this decade and throughout the next.

Every detail was important. Highly successful advertising featured humor based on empathy. A dramatic color scheme and logo—brazen purple, orange, and white—identified the company visually on planes, trucks, envelopes, and print advertising. Among employees, Smith stressed politeness, personal grooming, and the Protestant work ethic.

However, as Robert A. Sigafoos, author of *Absolutely Positively Overnight: The Story of Federal Express,* points out, had the corporate headquarters been located in a large city, even Smith's highly skilled powers of persuasion and leadership could have been overwhelmed by the forces against him. Organized labor would have been much more persistent and gotten a more sympathetic ear from employees. Urban workers would have been more cynical, less idealistic, preconditioned toward Smith's message than workers raised and educated in the cul-de-sac of Tennessee, Arkansas, and Mississippi.

Unshackled by business jargon, Smith's terms were colorful and clear. He likened stages of planning to the life cycle of a butterfly: caterpillar, into chrysallis, into butterfly. One memo Sigafoos cites was entitled, "Holding on to the Tiger's Tale," a forceful appeal for change. Smith often emphasized his arguments for change with aphorisms:

> What once were attributes can and will become serious detriments in the future. 'Che' was essential to Cuba *until* it was liberated. [Juan] Trippe built Pan Am and stayed long enough to sow the seeds of its destruction. Patton was marvelous in war, a disaster in peace. . . . The price of not curing the disease will be considerable. Emotion and ego satisfaction are a luxury that Federal Express cannot afford.[9]

Today, Federal Express is a visible success, but competition is keen. Public relations supplies a competitive advantage. It touts Federal as a larger company than Purolator Courier in terms of revenue. Less known is that Purolator carries 52 million overnight packages—as opposed to Federal's 38 million—at drastically lower rates. Federal must also overcome the fact that it is an unproven business concept operating nationally from an unlikely geographic area, Memphis. (This assessment by Sigafoos may overlook the fact that innovative growth industries such as Holiday Inns share the Memphis location, and that enterprise often comes from the rim land, not from the entrenched, conservative forces at the center.)

In a time of tangled, pallid corporate prose—often laden with weasel words, mugwump reasoning, and hide-bound thinking, Smith's marketing and communications are bold, refreshing, and at times audacious—a competitive asset.

## Creating the Craze for Cabbage Patch Dolls

Profited-oriented executives make two stinging criticisms of communicators: they cannot quantify their contributions and they shoot from the hip. Both are too often true.

Unlike marketing or product publicity, which can demonstrate increased sales volume or heightened public attention, corporate communications seldom translate into dollars earned. Essentially damage control, communications successes are conveniently forgotten once a threat is past. Often demonstrable value is possible only in the long term. Communicators must possess the same patient faith as teachers waiting years for students to demonstrate their capabilities. When corporate communications can produce hard figures—a costly strike averted, potentially costly legislation mutated or killed—they milk that one shining achievement throughout their careers.

The charge of shooting from the hip is equally unfair and just as well grounded. It stems from the conflicting demands, deadline pressures, and even personal styles between the operating executives, who strategize six months to five years out and managers of corporate city rooms, who must respond immediately to media opportunities and questions. Hip shooting may be the most efficient, perhaps only way, to handle volatile media relations.

Sometimes a case demonstrates that communicators can plan long range and produce a profit. The highly successful Cabbage Patch Kids fever was "created" cooperatively by the manufacturers, Coleco Industries; their advertising agency, Richard & Edwards; and their outside public relations counsel, Richard Weiner, Inc. What began as a $100,000 public relations campaign to promote offbeat looking dolls quickly became a masterstroke of marketing communications.

The distinctively ugly—the more charitable may say homely—kids caricatured their owners: plump, with straight, stubby arms and legs; squashed, ovoid heads; small, close-together eyes; and uniformly blank expressions. Almost antiheros, they represent real people, warts and all. And they require lots of care and loving. But how would they appeal to a society infatuated by beauty?

First, in-depth research explored the psychological and emotional aspects of looks and adoption. Richard Weiner, president of RWI, sought the counsel of child psychologists, pediatricians, early childhood educators, even a doll historian. Focus groups tested their suggestions.

The selling points emphasized the dolls' homely but huggable likeness to real babies; appealed to nurturing instincts, parental responsibility, and loving qualities. We learned, Weiner explained, that children do not consider themselves beautiful; that their parenting nature is aroused more by homely than by glamorous dolls.

In January 1983 the dolls were introduced in a "hospital nursery" at the American Toy Fair. By summer, mass adoptions were staged at press gatherings in several cities. Extensive trade press and general media interest—the *Today* and *Tonight* shows, a six-page spread and cover in *Newsweek*, and a *Wall Street Journal* editorial—fueled the moppet mania.

Supporting the media attention were promotions. A fourteen-page *Cabbage Patch Kids Parenting Guide*, featuring photos of children with their adoptees, gave practical advice on how to tie shoelaces and cross a street safely. Each owner became a member of the Cabbage Patch Kids Parents' Association. Accessories—fold-up carriers, slumber bags, and extensive wardrobe choices—increased sales.

Coleco ran no print advertisements; television commercials were shown only on Saturday mornings and in early evening, fringe hours. Even so, *Ad Week* claimed the public relations coup, crediting advertising for pushing the demand for the dolls beyond the supply.

If the publicity worked exactly according to plan—exceeding even Weiner's expectations—the shortages it produced caught everyone by surprise. Christmas shoppers fought and clawed their way to the few remaining dolls. Faced with this unusual but potentially damaging problem, Weiner and Coleco suspended advertising, but continued the publicity program. Coleco speeded production and delivery; offered dolls as prizes at charitable and public interest events.

The entire campaign, Weiner explains, was researched, developed, and executed for less than $500,000. It produced profits estimated between $50 and $60 million in 1983. Even so, Weiner notes, public relations is still viewed skeptically by media and some businesspeople; is still associated with chanciness. Many considered the craze a lucky fluke; others wanted the same excitement created for their products.[10]

Communicators planned, strategized, and produced continuing profits, benefits, and attention. New sizes, shapes, and costumes—twins, world travelers, ponies, dolls with a first tooth and glasses—were introduced. And the dolls still attract national publicity. When an orthodontist in Arlington, Texas, began gluing metal on the mouths of Cabbage Patch dolls as he put braces on the teeth of the dolls' owners it was reported widely.

Cabbage Patch mania was born again during the 1985 Christmas shopping season on Fifth Avenue in New York. Babyland, the new store (birthing facility) is a clinical study in marketing motherhood and Orwellian abuse of language.

The store is packaged with sales help (nurses and doctors) in full uniform, a special delivery stork, adoption cubicles where prospective customers (adoptive parents) pledge their care and pay adoption fees. Nostalgia was abundant—an old-fashioned country store and Dickens-like carolers in the windows. Men and women, old and young, stared at the windows, enraptured.

But the pièce de résistance is the Cabbage Patch itself. A salesperson (doctor) scrubbed, put on fresh gloves, and felt the cabbage heads. When the mother cabbage dilated to open four leaves, he announced that another kid was about to be born.[11] An unusual coup for communicators.

## Aloha to Puna Sugar

Sugar is an emotionally laden product, a way of life rather than merely a cash crop to the thousands who work all their lives in Hawaii's cane fields or mills—often as their fathers and grandfathers did before them. Sugar, with tourism and the military, dominates the state's economy.

The Americana of Hawaii is leavened by many unique influences: the Japanese, Chinese, Polynesians, Hawaiians, Haoles, and a mixture of just about every other people on earth. By optimism bred in a seeming paradise of constantly warm weather and sunshine. By the heritage of great courage demonstrated by those who sailed enormous distances across the South Pacific in primitive outriggers. Hawaiian terms infuse business discussions in Honolulu as Yiddish does in New York. And decisions tend to be made more meditatively, with wider participation, than on the mainland.

Sugar's many and intractable problems severely impact the state and its companies, including the largest, Amfac—a $2 billion diversified corporation. The state's leading private sector employer (10,000 employees), it produces almost one-third of Hawaii's crop. In the United States, sugar depends on government price supports, which cannot be counted on forever. Cane can be grown amost everywhere—from cold Scandinavian countries to southern Argentina and most places in between—usually more cheaply than in Hawaii.

Compounding these problems are changing tastes, a world sugar glut, nutritional activists, falling prices, and disappearing tariff barriers. The United States market is declining rapidly: from 101 pounds per capita in the early 1960s to 70 pounds in 1984, and still falling. Sugar no longer sweetens canned and bottled beverages—high-fructose corn sweeteners do it more cheaply.

Faced with these realities and high production costs, Amfac decided it must close its least efficient plantation, the Puna Sugar Company on the Big Island (Hawaii). At one time it covered 32,000 acres and employed 3,000 people. In 1982, Puna was losing $10 million annually. Losses were projected to double over the next two years, although closing would not end the losses, it would cut them substantially.

Few Hawaiians were surprised, but economic reality stunned. Local legislators considered any shutdown to be catastrophic, a severe blow to the economic health of the Hilo area, where most of Puna's 500 employees lived. This first plantation closing since Kohala in 1972 seemed to portend other shutdowns. Even so, when Amfac made its case candidly and sympathetically, legislators, trade union officials, and the community supported the action.

Henry A. Walker, Jr., at the time Amfac's president and CEO, today its chairman, sought the cooperation of everyone involved to make a painful necessity understandable and to cushion its effects as much as possible. Included were Governor George Ariyoshi, the United States congressional delegation, community councils, local legislators, affected employees, land-owners, other companies, and Hawaii Department of Agriculture officials. Walker estimated that "hundreds of thousands of hours" had been devoted to Puna's problems when the closing was announced. Everyone sensed that what in 1982 was Amfac's problem, tomorrow would be another grower's and Hawaii's.

At a news conference hosted by the governor in the state capitol, he noted: "The coming together today of labor, government and management demonstrates that sugar is everybody's business. We must work together to ease the pain."

Walker detailed the exhaustive evaluation of Amfac's sugar operations, aimed at cutting current and anticipated sugar losses on all its plantations. The conclusion: Puna had to be closed, phased out over a two-year period ending in 1984 to allow for harvesting crops already in the ground and for an orderly economic transition.

Congressman Daniel Akaka commented that if the closing signaled a trend in Hawaii, "then no one's life in this state will remain unchanged." He urged a new partnership in sugar: federal, state, industry, and labor interests.

Labor was involved in discussions from the beginning, as Amfac sought alternative opportunities for displaced workers—raising mangos, papaya, or other fruit, macadamia nuts, exotic flowers, biomass fuels, and feed grains—or relocation to other plantations.

The greatest innovation and generosity, however, was the gift of five acres of Puna land to each eligible employee to work as he chose. Arable land is exceedingly precious and scarce in Hawaii. The company also donated $2 million, plus road work equipment, to a nonprofit corporation to be devoted to, owned, and operated by employees. The company sought no financial assistance from any government agency, only cooperation to ameliorate the impact of Puna's wind-down and to help the Hawaiian sugar industry, even more embattled today, to survive.

At the news conference, ILWU President Tommy Trask said, "If there is any hope in this situation, it lies in Amfac's program, in its openness and sense of corporate responsibility." Some attendees were understandably skeptical about workers converting from large-scale farming to cottage agriculture, but Trask explained that the majority were experienced farmers who could adapt quickly and well. Others questioned the land gift: No propaganda? No strings attached? Walker assured them all the land would be contributed just as soon as the maze of zoning, legal, and other considerations was worked through.

Amfac's proposal ran a cropper of government restrictions and other conditions, principally county zoning and development costs. Eventually, the most workers had to pay was $20,000 for the one acre they could receive — still a bargain for scarce, valuable Hawaiian land. Another stumbling block was revealed by a University of Hawaii survey of Puna Sugar employees. Eighty-one percent said that they did not want to farm.

Even this unusual cooperation has not cured sugar's ills. However, its plight became well understood through Amfac's extensive public relations program based on grassroots, community involvement. In 1981, Amfac, facing heavy losses ($30 million that year alone), used all means of formal and informal communications to dramatize the sugar industry's historic and contemporary importance to Hawaii. A day-long Save Our Sugar (SOS) rally was attended by almost 10,000 people in a Honolulu park.

*Pau hana* (the end) came for Puna on September 19, 1984. A somber, ceremonial caravan of fifteen cane trucks — the lead one piled high with the final load of cane, the other big rigs empty — wound their way down Volcano Highway to the mill. Drivers tooted their air horns; it sounded like a giant horde of bumble bees amplified many times. Employees, many with no solid job prospects, gathered to watch the final unloading. They had worked hard to the very end so the mill would be closed with dignity. As the unloading began, someone inside the factory dropped a few gallons of crude oil into the boiler. Suddenly a thick, black column arose from the smokestack. A death pall over the dying sugar mill and the only industry Puna had ever known. Just an hour later, Kilauea erupted, sending a thick column of lava almost 1,000 feet into the air. Its red fountaining could be seen throughout the Puna district.

The lessons of this Pacific Rim action? Many executives expect — and experience — only labor–management antagonism. Even in times of genuine economic hardship and drastically diminished markets, appeals to workers' sense of fairness and intelligence can produce beneficial results to everyone.[12] Sugar workers and the community, because of the extensive communications efforts, understood how threatened all their futures were by declining acreage, lower prices, and endangered supports. Puna demonstrates how cooperation of labor, government, and company, how open and candid communication, can make the best of a dim present and perhaps an even more difficult future.

# 8

# Understanding the
# Janus Manager

## *Communicators in Corporations*

Wanted

CEO seeks corporate communications officer. Duties: keep media at bay; explain company's prospects to financial community and individual shareholders; function as corporate undertaker to come in after the fact to explain lapses and tout successes; motivate employees; feed executive egos. Qualifications: communications/media background desired but not required; legal, financial, or operating skills preferred; must have informed world view, but understand management and marketing. Evaluation: based on personal chemistry and perceptions. Prospects: large department budget and staff, subject to severe cutting and dismemberment in tight times; high visibility with other members of senior management and public enhances career opportunities.

Who would answer this preposterous advertisement? Most communications officers for major corporations. They know, but usually don't voice, that this description more pragmatically summarizes their responsibilities than all the wishful mush written in trade journals and management guides or mouthed by company recruiting sergeants.

Denigration of corporate communicators is both great sport and popular, but senior managers indulge in it at high risk. Many recent disasters—damaging to companies in dollars, public support, employee loyalty, and product preference—involved public perceptions, media relations, and communications. Dalkon Shield, companies hiding deleterious effects of new pharmaceuticals, Bhopal, and public fights among senior executives—even Tylenol, an image and marketing success—all cost dearly. When the public or media focus on an issue, such as toxic waste disposal, when it's a hot topic, only absolute honesty and complete correction succeed. Good communicators know this, but must demonstrate it again and again to naturally skeptical managements, often by recounting cautionary tales from corporate battle-fields. Here's one from Waste Management, the nation's largest disposal firm. In March 1985, a former employee made front-page headlines by tell-ing how the company had illegally disposed of toxic chemicals at an Ohio dump site. In two days, shares dropped thirty percent. Waste Management feared its name was sullied forever, that government fines and extensive liti-gation would cut into its highly profitable thirty percent operating margins.

It reacted aggressively in appearance and operations by creating an envi-ronmental compliance department beefing up internal controls and lobbying efforts, and launching a $5 million television advertising campaign. These actions impressed investors. Even though executives admitted past lapses: significant reporting delays, mishandling, and storage problems—they won-dered why the EPA seemed to deliberately scrutinize and penalize the com-pany, to make it a public example. These executives had fallen into the classic trap of not understanding that when an industry leader or business sector is under suspicion, cosmetics can't conceal. Public relations, lobbying, even chopping executive heads is not enough. Nothing less than radical surgery—complete clean-up—will do.

No communications officer makes himself popular by bearing such tid-ings; nor does he enhance his credibility by having to rely on projections, hunches, or soft reasoning. Tough-minded number crunchers and operations people don't want production mucked up by some might-bes. Many com-municators further weaken their position by not even trying to think in terms of their peers. Unlike other managers, communicators do not have the force of established procedures, such as legal codes or production statistics, as a power base and substantiation. Rather, they must often rest their counsel on experience—usually only their own—plus opinions and judgments that are binding on absolutely no one. Even with a faultless track record, survival can be precarious.

As David Halberstam describes in *The Best and the Brightest*, quantifiers in the Pentagon documented, with apparently incontrovertible evidence, the effectiveness of bombing runs, body counts, and general Vietnam readiness. One querulous fellow over in a corner recited a mantra like Herman Mel-ville's Bartleby: in my gut it seems wrong. He was discounted, fired, but eventually proven correct. Critical decisions well based in statistics, marketing surveys, and legal considerations, too often exclude or belatedly admit public perceptions, long-term ramifications, and communications considerations.

The communicator faces other difficulties unique to his function and background. While finance, law, operations, and marketing are venerated as fast internal tracks to the top, the communications officer often rises through liberal arts, media, and writing—outside the company. Those with purely communications education may suffer from training that was either too nuts-and-bolts or too theoretical. A recent Conference Board survey of 300 CEOs of major companies showed that sixty percent had been with their companies at least twenty-one years. The longevity customary among most executives is unusual in communications. While most other officers are Ivy League white males, the token woman or black often heads the communications department. It is too often abused as the dumping ground for corporate losers, burn-outs easing into retirement, or badly trained liberal arts graduates who "like people" but are otherwise unfocused.

Insufficient information or candor from the top is another difficulty. Some practitioners depict themselves as mushrooms: kept in the dark, and shoveled shit. The communicators' credo seems to be "last to know; first to go." Even the most competent are excluded from the inner ring of information and influence, where secrecy produces great power. One street-smart woman officer lacked access to rumors regularly posted on the mirror in the executives men's room, until female cleaners leveled the advantage. Not being informed fosters adamant ego-touting attitudes that irritate colleagues. Even well-trained communicators, unfortunately, adopt standoffish, even elitist, stances or slight the guts and realities of the business. In one major company, the communications department—from the vice president down— made a point of professional pride never to attend a marketing meeting, talk over plans with brand managers, or come down from their lofty professional perches to walk a plant floor. When a tough, cost-conscious management took over, almost the entire department was fired—and they were not missed. Only those who demonstrated their value survived.

Communicators can be handicapped by a different sense of urgency, priorities, and timing than other executives. To operating managers who are developing five-year business plans or writing twenty-year insurance policies, other deadlines seem rude and unrealistic. Break into a planning meeting on marketing in the 1990s when the press is clamoring for a statement on an oil spill and criticism is sure to follow—the statement will come only much later.

Unlike the corporate structure, the news room environment—media or company—allows little time to talk about strategic planning. A communicator faces what he is assigned or what erupts. He must be prepared, organizationally and personally, for the single event, the one telephone call that can transform a company's relative normalcy into a maelstrom, a rush of event and tensions. This unique view can be excellent training for a business career—it was for this author. While many senior managers of large corporations were attending prep school and later prestigious universities and graduate schools, the author already was immersed in a demanding newspaper city room. There was no talk of strategic planning. Reporters faced what they were assigned: a church fire in the morning and a senator's speech in the evening sandwiching a lady-lady luncheon. Instead of cheering for the home team, the author was watching highway accidents and sniffing out the shady backroom deals of small-town politicians. Abrupt change, adversarial situations, and searching out facts in mazes of contradictions were drilled into the author's journalistic psyche early—and were put to good corporate use later.

Investigations and almost engulfing, microscopic media attention can magnify existing small fault lines into deep crevices and can damage promising careers. Most executives, basically very private and highly organized individuals, are put off by the hurly-burly turbulence of the corporate city room and the media's uncontrollable demands and deadlines. Even with insight and planning, a great deal of effort is expended in responding to events that erupt suddenly. Some of these a novice will smile over incredulously. But any seasoned communicator can trade war stories about suicides, blackmail, expropriations or illegal payments; bailing out a homosexual executive; explaining why a boss died in the wrong bed with the wrong woman; cleaning up a publicly messy marital situation; or disclaiming any connection between an executive falling downstairs, fatally breaking his neck and major investigations of his company.

Business school graduates and fast-trackers to the contrary, no single recipe guarantees success. Communications officers, perhaps more than any others, must be sensitive, astute Januses—very much involved internally in the business, as well as consummately versed in marketing and general strategies.[1] They must be able to translate the hard-knuckles world of media relations to colleagues, and to spot specks on the horizon potentially important to the company. They must be multidimensional thinkers who do not ape their peers—who are willing to tactfully ask the tough questions that others may be too political, polite, or uninformed to ask.

What is needed is not just a yeoman who can make a great media buy, create a zingy commercial, write a speech, or plant a favorable story in a home town newspaper. That's expected and minor. More important are acute awareness of cross currents of public opinion; an understanding not just of the techniques of communications, but of the overriding issues; and knowledge not just of short-range tactics, but of strategies that may make or break the company. Such wide-vision thinkers must also be as adaptable as the character Dustin Hoffman played in *Tootsie*, who was desperate for any role.

## Founders and Followers

The founders of public relations were as heterogeneous a collection of personalities as their heirs, today's practitioners. Edward Bernays, Sigmund Freud's nephew, introduced sociological and psychological tools to influence public opinion. John W. Hill was a canny Indiana farmboy with a genius for seeing the profitable niche and understanding current needs; Milton Fairman, a Chicago newspaper man, built one of the first major corporate departments at Borden, Inc. Harold Burson came north to New York from Memphis with newspaper and counseling skills to chair Burson Marsteller. Chester Burger, manager and counselor from Brooklyn, developed the unique role of confidential advisor to CEOs and leading public relations and advertising firms. None practiced public relations in the almost mindless, nitty-gritty manner of many fictional stereotypes.

Just as Bernays identified opportunities for publicity high jinks, and Hill the importance of labor–management strife immediately following World War II, their progressive followers today are matching their efforts to the temper of new times. Astute practitioners understand how vital communications can be in an age of multinational labor forces and stiffer competition; wider use of visual than print communication, particularly with employees; less management layering; downsizing of organizations; and greater participation by the people who actually make, assemble, or sell products. That said, communicators still must make managements realize how vital an accurate, respected public understanding is to corporate profitability—even to survival.

Public relations is a very new trade; many of the founders trained today's senior practitioners. Although the past is seldom any prologue today, a brief look at how counselors and companies worked in the past, can enhance an understanding of the growing sophistication and seriousness evident today.

No complex event can be satisfactorily pinpointed as starting at a precise moment or by a single pioneer, but it is generally agreed that Bernays and his work in 1918 with the United States Committee on Public Information introduced press agentry. Those who first worked with Bernays were authors, newspaper and advertising men, and college professors, who scrambled for information wherever they could. Chief executives in both government and business were reluctant then—as some still are today—to court public opinion. An opportunity was lost to gain support for the Treaty of Versailles when President Woodrow Wilson refused, despite prodding, to engage in popular activities that would delight American newspaper readers.

In the 1920s, as public relations began expanding rapidly, companies hired staff regardless of experience. Much was trial and error. Press gimmicks abounded. For a client, Bernays countered the new fashion of shingled hair styles, which did away with hair nets, by publicizing appearance, safety, and health reasons for continuing to wear nets. He was convincing. For example, everyone cooking in a restaurant or working in a factory was required to wear a net regardless of hair length.

Another Bernays coup was Ivory soap recognition. He staged a cleanliness campaign and arranged publicity events like washing public statues and sculpturing soap. His most spectacular success—unthinkable today—was for the American Tobacco Company. To change the déclassé image of cigarette smoking, Bernays established a Tobacco Society of Voice Culture, Inc.: "So to improve the chords of the throat through cigarette smoking that the public will be able to express itself in songs of praise and more easily to swallow anything. . . . Our ultimate goal: A smoking teacher for every singer."[2]

The publicist touted cigarettes not as a pleasure, but as medicine. He sought and got testimonials from physicians. Appealing to weight-conscious women, he urged, "Reach for a Lucky instead of a sweet," To enhance the female market—nice women then did not smoke freely and surely not publicly—he induced New York City debutantes to parade on Easter along Fifth Avenue obviously smoking. Discovering a female preference for green, the packaging was redesigned accordingly.

Unfortunately, this early era left impressions that still plague public relations today: slick press agents, hidden persuaders, devious manipulators of dummy fronts organizations and golden livers, who expensively ply the power brokers and media with drinks and favors. But image lags behind the reality. Business is too serious and abstemious, and the media is too sensitive to accept even a token gift and too health-minded to indulge in drinking orgies.

## Use and Abuse of Communications

The Great Depression boosted public relations. Responding to widespread criticism of capitalism, business realized it could no longer merely sell its goods and services. It had to explain its broader contribution to society. A book written in 1957 by John W. Hill, founder and long-time intellectual force behind Hill and Knowlton, expanded this mandate, setting the stage for a widening and professionalizing of communications.[3] To Hill, public relations had no mystical powers to work miracles, sway public opinion, or create lasting value where none existed. Rather, communications was a broad management function rooted in integrity, soundness of policies, decision making, and actions able to be viewed in the light of public interest.

Hill's counsel succeeded because it suited the times. As labor and management struggled, he told management that employees were its nearest and most important audience. Lukewarm communications with them, or any other public, was worse than none. Nor could smart publicity ever replace sound management policies and good financial results in building a lasting foundation of good will. People must know what a company is doing to approve of its actions. If management refuses to tell its own story, someone else will—probably incorrectly. Too many managements bestir themselves to tackle a problem only at its flash point, Hill continued. Then, confounded by slow-moving public attitudes and seemingly intractable problems, they grow frustrated and bored, leaving the field open to the unrelenting efforts of detractors. Hill espoused a different approach: once companies are sure policies are right and decent, that their house is clean of pay-offs and other possible embarrassments, then they should tell the story forthrightly and repeatedly. As George Cabot Lodge wrote later, Hill told private enterprise that it exists only under the franchise of public opinion.

Perhaps the best-known, although somewhat misleading picture of public relations in its earlier years is *The Man in the Gray Flannel Suit*, which has passed into public consciousness as synonymous with conformity. Actually, the central figure of Sloan Wilson's novel was struggling to adapt himself from the relative security of olive drab to the quicksand world of late-1940s corporate public relations. In his interview for a public relations job at United Broadcasting Corporation, he gave expected, not truthful, answers: Why do you want to work for UBC? It's a good company, not for the money. Why PR? Not merely because the job is open, but because my previous experience at a foundation would be helpful. However, one question hasn't changed since then: Can you write?

Although he hated the work, he dredged up the expected enthusiasm for researching "nauseatingly noble" speeches for a mental health committee that his chairman sought to ride to fame. "If you want good publicity, do something good." Friends predicted a great future in publicity, because he was already defending his boss from all comers and criticism. "We don't write speeches for Mr. Hopkiss. We just help him with the research—take notes on the great man's thoughts and try to get something on paper for him to work with."

Ghostwriting still daunts communicators. Viewed as a specialized service, it is not a pathway to power unless the writer develops a unique rapport with senior officers or is perceived within the organization as having special entrée. Even the most skillful ghost finds it an intimidating, intimate exercise to catch an executive's thoughts exactly or coax them from him. The writer must phrase the thoughts comfortably, with appropriate allusions to golf, military or fishing and avoid tongue-tangling phrases. If the writer has far different experiences and purview, the collaboration succeeds only if the officer shares his ideas initially, then works closely with the writer so the words and thoughts appear to be the officer's.

Public relations in the 1950s—the world in which Wilson's character operated—seems almost innocent and secretarial to us now. Checking out hotel arrangements: Was the mattress hard? Did long-stemmed roses grace the night table? Were the meeting room lectern and notebooks ready? Was the press alerted to receive the news release? The hacks, who give communications a menial image, still work on that level. However, even sophisticated, seasoned professionals get immersed in such ludicrous, time-consuming tasks. They always look deceptively easy, but never are.

Sloan Wilson's man learned early that whistle-blowing, or even less than the most robust support, is translated as disloyalty. "I'll always tend to agree, until I get big enough to be honest without being hurt. That's not being crooked, it's just being smart." Saying anything for pay. But like petting a tiger, one must be very careful. Even today, liabilities for bearing bad news or disagreeing are still high, except with the most self-assured, progressive managers. As a result of polite silence, many problems are hidden when nascent, only to blossom into major magnitude later. An ethicist recounts a meeting during which a manager explored his responsibility for red-flagging the dangers of a chemical. Everyone attending pooh-poohed its importance, saying it was neither ethical nor necessary to bring the matter to a superior's attention. The chemical was kepone, which soon after the meeting became a major environmental and publicity problem.[4]

Thomas McCann, for many years United Fruit's vice president of public relations, traces communications from the company's go-go years through its public meddling in Central American politics, and finally to the abuses by Chairman Eli Black.[5] Before his very public suicide in 1975, he turned publicity into personal vanity and created financial Potemkin villages that even savvy newspaper men believed.[6]

Bernays began counseling the company by suggesting a Middle American Information Bureau, financed and run within United Fruit. To complement his work, an internal department was created in 1955; within a year its staff grew to twenty-eight, with a budget of $1.5 million. One highly visible project was an institutional advertising campaign, "The Living Circle," run in Spanish-language publications. The great wheel was superimposed on a map of America. From the north came an endless supply of all good things: cars, refrigerators, radios, television sets, tires, and other manufactured products. From the south came all the materials and agricultural products one could take from the land; raw rubber, minerals, lumber, and especially bananas. A graphic although unwitting representation of colonialism. Even in that less-sensitized time, the campaign created resentment and rancor in Central America. Typically, the company was so isolated from the impact of its actions and attitudes that it continued the advertising for almost five years, inflaming its audiences and working counter to any conceivable self-interest.

Other weaknesses illustrated by United Fruit's efforts—a cautionary tale for any practitioner—involved erecting facades, inspiring chimeras, and attempting to maneuver public figures for self-interest. When problems arose with union activist Ceasar Chavez, for example, corporate managers insisted on a public stance of cooperation with the United Fruit Workers Union, despite earlier animosity. Black tried maladroitly to "handle Chavez" by inviting him to participate in a well-attended religious service. "That's PR," crowed Black. But all the publicity and fellowship in the world are worthless when each side must represent his constituencies.

Despite United Fruit's well-known record in Central America, company films attempted to position it as the hemisphere's most enlightened benefactor. But the incongruity of photographs showing freshly laundered T-shirts on exuberantly happy workers and faked blow-ups of the plantations mocked the accuracy. When a more honest attempt was aimed at college students, Black tried to kill it.

Such public relations efforts featured many techniques accepted then by company, press, and public. Junkets to the tropics were conducted for reporters, who saw only company-staged events. United Fruit sponsored newspapers, circulated free to employees, often their only source of information. Here, too, the company misjudged. Many employees were illiterate; others railed at the refusal to discuss issues and the paper's portrayal of life on a banana plantation as an idyllic, happy holiday. Soon the newspapers were supplanted by inexpensive transistor radios even the poorest employee could afford. Radios provided more information than company-sponsored publications. No reporter, CEO, or communications officer with a smattering of brains would even attempt any of these tactics today.

## Crazing the Communicator

No corporate officer is as vulnerable to executive ego, to foibles and excesses, as the communicator. Personal chemistry is vital not only because of the communicator's responsibilities, but also because of the nature of the working relationship. Yet, crazy bosses, like ego, are usually ignored, or at best smiled over sympathetically, when recounted to the battle-wise. At worst, corporate novices may greet such tales with disbelief, or even question the teller's balance. Pathological superiors—workaholics, those who wishfully indulge in appearances rather than reality, those who operate and judge according to religious and sexual prejudices, those who suffer serious but overlooked or unrecognized personality flaws, those who focus on unimportant details rather than crux issues—wreak great damage, especially on communicators. Every executive has his own stock of Captain Queeg-like yarns. The stories that follow all actually happened; each illustrates a liability particular to corporate communications.

*Appearances.* In a time when packaging is paramount, when snap judgments are made on appearance and office alone, a typewriter can be dangerous to success. One highly respected communicator was ruled out of a promotion to officer because he had a typewriter in his office and, worse yet, actually used it. The successful candidate, whose office in another company also housed a typewriter, was very careful not to move one into the executive suite. Women executives are reluctant to have a word processor or anything roughly resembling a typewriter around: too close to the secretarial stigma.

*Incidentals That Win.* Every communicator knows that he may stand or fall on whether he gets an executive's daughter's wedding announcement in *The New York Times* or *Washington Post* society page, secures scarce tickets for the superbowl, knows the "in" restaurants or plays, or arranges an honorary degree or a coveted speaking engagement. One chairman, very skeptical about communications, finally warmed up. His great idea—and it was—was to strike a commemorative plate with an attractive annual report cover design.

*Illegalities.* During the height of sensitive, intense national investigations of a company, a corporate loser sought to regain power by controlling media relations. Talking to reporters looks like great fun, power, and visibility to the uninitiated executive who has never been backed into a corner by a smart reporter or misquoted in headlines and then had to explain them. To accomplish his aims, the executive had to defeat and/or neutralize the press chief. What better means than taping, secretly, a planted incriminating interview? However, the communicator defended himself long and comprehensively enough that the hidden tape buzzed its presence.

*Prejudice.* Even today, when management should be objective, communicators get unsolicited prejudiced advice. Be a journalist from New York City and read books and you'll be cautioned about the local difficulties of being Jewish. He wasn't. Sign a pro-abortion petition published in a newspaper and be counseled about how serious it is for a Roman Catholic to go public against church teaching. She wasn't. Have lunch in an eating club frequented by officer peers with a long-time friend and be counseled against being seen there again with a black. He was.

*Yes, But.* Communicators are charged with understanding how the media works. But the media's demand for information may be at cross purposes with legal counsel. Even the most convincing communicator may lose his case until the next day's headlines. One company under intense scrutiny by investigative reporters wanted to stonewall them. Lawyers won; communicators lost. The next day, when management was wooing financial analysts, a long, uncomplimentary story written without company input ran on page one.

*Women, Still a Special Case.* The first senior management opportunity for many women frequently comes in communications or human resources, often perceived as soft areas by machismo management. This poses additional difficulties, particularly if the woman has more street smarts than her male peers.[7] She is in a vulnerable post at best: she must bear bad news and counsel against some of the firmest-held ideas of others. This was *one* factor in Mary Cunningham's troubles at Bendix. When a woman appears with males at a meeting, even today, she is assumed to be a subordinate, never the boss, although only dolts still assume automatically that she is a secretary. One woman officer and a male who reported to her visited a corporate subsidiary. The guide assigned to them concentrated on the male; she was invisible. Finally, he asked very confidentially, "How does it feel to work for a broad?" "Meet her," the subordinate responded.

Another woman, the first on a posh executive floor, was barred one weekend from her office. The guards just knew no woman had an office there, and secretaries were not allowed up on weekends without special permission. Later, when her secretary asked for a key to the ladies' room for her, the response was ribald.

*Accreditation and Degrees.* Non-degree-holders may not be hired to push cheese in supermarkets, or a non-high school graduate who is a member of Mensa may not be considered for an audiovisual position he handled elsewhere successfully. But too many credentials are problems, too. APR, the sign of accreditation so important to public relations practitioners, means little or may even be negative to others. Ph.D.s are particularly suspect. What can a theoretically trained Ph.D. know about corporations, business, even communications? Lots. If a woman has a doctorate and her male superior does not, she should be ready for not-too-subtle suggestions to drop it.

## Fiction Illuminates Reality

James Baar, a sardonic and witty public relations man, gives very realistic insights into press and corporate information sources in his spoof *The Great Free Enterprise Gambit.* Business writers sit in a three-row semicircle in plush oversized conference chairs. Some, "dressed like bankers, carry pocket calculators, gold pencils and attaché cases"; they assume the mien of senior loan officers. "Others are rumpled and openly pugnacious. A few in business gray fawn nervously in hopes of future employment." Most smell trouble, happily anticipating their claims to major space for particularly nasty stories.

The CEO, expectedly, wants to cut a couple of those bastards off at the pockets. The vice president of corporate information, also typically, attempts to allay his boss's worries following a press conference with the canard of canards: "We can handle them. Believe me, I know those guys." Famous last words, uttered before the deluge of truth; the next day's headlines. One, reading "IC Rents Mercenary Troops to Latin American Dictators," produced a nightmare, a saturation attack of press calls. Predictably, hauling out a cannon to kill a gnat, the vice president of public information devised "operation integrity," to show up those crazy press sharpshooters who are printing all that rotten stuff. Usually, public relations people delight in seeing their company's name in headlines; in this instance it was depressing. To show "them" that the company was moving forward in the old IC spirit, a massive campaign was unfurled with great fanfare and at great expense. It was just ineffectual, laughable boilerplate.

In Baar's novel, the CEO explains away the company's difficult financial condition, saying that what look today like major setbacks tomorrow will be regarded as minor blips on the curve—an attitude that would make the Rock of Gibraltar look spongy, and arouses the possible worst suspicions. Fiscal fairy tales will return to haunt a company if financial performance does not fulfill public promises.

## What CEOs Should Expect of Communicators

Many senior managers, fully confident when evaluating other subordinates, puzzle over what to demand of the communications officer and how to assess his performance. Communication is a staff, not an operating function; a cost rather than a profit center; and is difficult to quantify in a numbers-dominated corporate culture. Most important, personalities vary greatly. Harry Gray of United Technologies to the contrary, most CEOs come to major responsibilities with modest contact with media or communications. The straddling of spheres—finding the commonality between communications and business strategy—is akin to bridging the gap between techies and more traditional managers. Communicators must know the business well enough to devise the most effective public positions, while the CEO must know operations intimately and enough about communications to view it as a valuable tool. Complicating this equation is a growing tendency to appoint communicators who are unschooled in their trade and unable to write well. (One concerned veteran writer, baffled by this trend, foresees sign language and semaphore.)

Ronald E. Rhody, a respected veteran practitioner and now senior vice president of the Bank of America, recently offered a public relations primer to young presidents.[8] No single group, he pointed out, gets as much sheer hokum thrown at them as CEOs, especially the newly appointed. Consultants, experts, professional ego-salvers, and many Monday morning quarterbacks—all of whom enjoy perfect 20/20 hindsight—second guess decisions and offer advice for fancy fees.

The worst, however, are the fuzzy futurists, infected with rampant overoptimism bred of never having carried profit and loss responsibilities, who encourage expensive, extensive, but nonproductive studies. The logic is impeccable, but not profitable. Many consultants mouth hot management fads—spin-off, merger, going private, leveraged buy-out, intrapreneurial—and shoe-horn them into any situation, regardless of applicability. All these off-target experts afflict the CEO more than any other corporate officer because he is viewed as being so powerful and yet much more susceptible to outside pressures.

Many CEOs, Rhody pointed out, stumble through the socioeconomic landscape in happy ignorance, bruising and sometimes even savaging customers, shareholders, and employees. This creates negative public perceptions that can result in lost markets, unproductive employees, restrictive if not punitive laws and regulations, and recruitment difficulties.

To be successful, Rhody advised managers to integrate all the forces operating in their environment, dealing with the emotions, fears, and expectations of all the publics they touch, not just those they choose to reach or even are aware of.[9] The surprises in business will not come from the closely monitored, well-known corporate heartlands, but from the rim lands: universities; social activists; previously silent, aggrieved *Rolling Stone* readers; patriotic but resentful rust belt towns; a lumpen proletariat who are seldom given a voice until a news event erupts in their midst. Often trouble brews outside the experience or purview of inwardly directed senior management. It should not surprise a broadly trained and interested public relations manager—although it does.

Rhody urged business leaders to manage in the future by consent and consensus, not command and control. To accomplish this, a CEO should expect his communications people to have these basic qualities:

- Skills in mass communications and interpersonal relations.

- Media expertise.

- A creative discipline.

- Standard and shared techniques in social science and political affairs.[10]

(A standard budget for a well-rounded program relates to company size and needs, but a sound yardstick is one-tenth to one-quarter of one percent of sales for larger established corporations.)

Publics act on their perceptions. How they view a company and its leaders, rightly or wrongly, is almost as important as what the company actually does. Short-term communications programs can help mitigate and preempt misleading information on issues important to the company. But over the long haul, it is important to build a climate of public opinion and understanding that will allow legislators, regulators, and the general public to support operations and positions vital to the company.

Corporate performance, no matter how stellar, never speaks loudly and accurately enough to cut through the cacophony and competition of noise from disparate sources. To make a persuasive or competitive difference, officers must be bold enough to tell of achievements aggressively and often.

In all this the CEO plays a critical role:

- He must be marketed skillfully. Although he may shrink from the unfamiliar and uncongenial public spokesman role, it is essential to project the corporate personality and to become a public asset with constituencies.

- Personal communications. Leaders must project confidence: be persuasive, authoritative, and articulate, speaking in the lingo of the constituencies. However, these appearances must be rationed to complement strategies and conserve executive time.

- Few CEOs have the time, and perhaps not even the talent, to write speeches, position papers, and testimony. Here an articulate writer can assist, but never take over.

- Communications policy. Rhody concludes that the media's all-pervasiveness, the instantaneousness of information, and the fish-bowl business environment make one point abundantly clear: nothing is secret. The only safe policy is to tell all the truth as fast and as accurately as possible.

Battle-like pressure hones principles about crisis coping and communications. The best, most valuable communicators must keep saying, "Look out that window to a wider world." And do it all while understanding the corporate culture well enough to keep their jobs.

# 9

# Paths Around Pitfalls

## *Avoiding Communications Disasters*

E ACH communications crisis is different; none has a set pattern and few have the desired quick and easy solution. As the cases commented on in this book indicate, sometimes the CEO can be too visible or too noticeably absent. Detailed advanced planning is almost sufficient in some instances, but in many sudden disasters it can be just an incomplete road map. Some aggrieved executives benefit from public protest; for others, it merely drags the story out and makes the executive sound like the proverbial misquoted politician. Some companies suffer by speaking out boldly; others have been hurt by being too quiet and defensive, even when basically in the right.

Just as managers thirst after Japanese recipes for success—rather than selectively adapting the most useful methods—managers under public pressure or in the throes of major turmoil, particularly for the first time, may seek the one quick fix. Be assured: there isn't any. But intelligent general planning, developing personal survival techniques, and making sure that operations and people don't fall into classic traps are essential.

First, scope the environment—honestly, not wishfully. Trace lines, in retrospect, are always so obvious. The challenge is to spot in advance those that will affect a company and to plan for or minimize their impact. Taking lessons from the best analytical work of good government intelligence agencies or sometimes simply tapping sources not normally used by competitors can yield an advantage. Letters of protest in *The New York Review of Books* indicated the Shah's shakiness long before it was evident in business publications. Another useful technique is borrowing from disciplines not usually applied to business problems. Historians, particularly of the Annales school, point out that the easily seen and understood surface events may not be the most important. By the time an event cracks through the surface it may already be less powerful and significant than the glacially moving, difficult to detect and understand events that are hidden under many layers. Often such events are simply overlooked.

Because dramatic changes often spring from unexpected sources, a manager will benefit from studying the lines of power at the periphery, as an indication of the future at the center. American historian Francis Parkman saw early on that the French empire in the New World was coming unstuck in the forest: first in the rimland, then at the heart.

Second, attempt to view the company as others do, particularly important audiences and the media. Adopt their mindset. Internal assumptions and procedures, the essential concentration of senior management on immediate, pressing business concerns dulls or delays the need to think of how an action will look to the public. I sensitized communicators to this by telling them to write a news release then to literally walk around to the other side of their desks and ask as an editor or reporter (most had been) what they would believe or find newsworthy. That's advice for the press as well as business.

Third, attempt to appreciate the often extreme pressures on the media: relentless deadlines—particularly on television and wire services—an equally relentless appetite for dramatic news and photographs, and fierce competition. Also, media people may be coming to your story tired, having just covered a totally different subject. Business people and journalists share tough, exacting work in a high-pressure world where mistakes are dealt with harshly, but often this common condition is overlooked.

Fourth, hire a pragmatic, wide-vision thinker as the communications officer, then let him operate. Appreciate that, more than others reporting to the CEO, he must be a hybrid—very much a business, internal type, consummately versed in market and business realities, but also able to translate for colleagues the hard-knuckled needs of media relations and the less-controllable public arena. If he is excluded from the ring of information, but expected to front for the company, he is sure to transmit that lack to a vigilant press. To succeed—as executive or department—communications must be part of the corporation's total activities: built into long-range strategic plans, not patched in as an afterthought or peripheral activity. Some communicators call themselves corporate undertakers, people who are invited in after the death or damage.

The human toll of corporate turmoil is too often overlooked. That attitude may be popular, upbeat, and machismo, but it may leave the individual unprepared. The sound, pragmatic management skills that have gained an executive senior corporate rank will help him succeed in time of crisis. However, he must devise his own individual ways of keeping his footing and balance, his humor and perspective, while the maelstrom whirls about him—a psychological gyroscope. Theoreticians in stress management have their nostrums. Those who have been in the trenches themselves have others, probably of greater utility when events heat up. A circle of confidants, people one can truly trust and who have shared roughly similar experiences, spells survival. Talking to the most intelligent, most well-intentioned family or friends can be a little like the experience of soldiers on home leave from the Western Front during World War I. Despite the gunfire occasionally heard booming in the distance, despite the awesome losses, the soldiers' tales of battlefield horror were met with incredulity. Even several years after the Armistice, Vera Brittain, a front line nurse, was treated as a little eccentric by students who were unscathed.

It also helps to have experienced observers who can assure the executive under public fire that others have survived such plights, and that his, too, will end eventually. He may not totally believe them, however. Some surprises in events and people will be nasty, but others will be unexpectedly pleasant. The personal qualities most essential to survival are patience, doggedness, and the willingness to go on—day by weary day, revelation by revelation, leak by leak, misstatement by misstatement. Even so, the best communicators and best executives are not always the winners.

Three of the most common pitfalls—which seem so obvious until you find yourself making them—are:

First, running operations as if the public were not interested. Aggressive reporters; greater interest in business news generally and in personalities perceived to be powerful, successful, and exciting; government investigations; and the general distrust of institutions leave nothing private for very long today. Expecting that even a relatively routine action by a major company—particularly if it involves jobs, product safety, or the environment—will not arouse media interest is foolhardy. And secrets always surface at the most damaging, inconvenient, and embarrassing times.

When in doubt about an action, do as Dick Cheney of Hill and Knowlton suggests and write a release explaining why it was taken. Often that is enough. Or, be just a bit more dramatic—but not much—if you are a defense contractor or chemical company and ask how that operational lapse, decision-making procedure, or product weakness would look on the front page of the *Washington Post* or on network television night after night. What is the cost analysis of public prudence beforehand compared to staggering costs later?

The second obvious pitfall is poisoning the in box. Bad news gets strained out as it goes up the chain of command, as was tragically demonstrated by the *Challenger* disaster. No one wants to tell the boss it won't work, it's dangerous, or even to consider a worst-case scenario. Strong language blurs into compromising weasel words that are easily misunderstood and interpreted for one's own purpose. To counter this, sincerely encourage a management milieu that is open to loyal, intelligent disagreement. Ask for dissenting or minority opinions in memos and for the various reasons on which a decision was based, rather than accepting a bland, hopeful consensus that may conceal major questions and disagreements. Among communicators there is a saying: They're rearranging the deck chairs on the *Titanic,* but no one's on iceberg watch.

Encouraging a trusted devil's advocate to hone thoughts also helps to depoison the in box. No one is smart enough to be his own devil's advocate. More intensive supervision and investigation by shoe leather balance the staff-generated information on which decisions are based. Unconventional means may be the most rewarding, but also the most disconcerting and overlooked. One health care executive thought that it would be flaky to visit pioneering storefront health maintenance operations. Hospice was suspect, too. He closed his mind to the visits and, unfortunately for his company, to a substantial piece of future business.

The third common pitfall is unrehearsed spokespeople. They are perilous, particularly at a press conference or in times of crises, when an executive confronts the press prepared only with his untested self-confidence and enthusiasm for a project or point of view. Lacking precision of expression, he may oversell a solution or a product. It is also perilous to the job security of the communicator who tries to forewarn the uncooperative spokesperson about the tough, embarrassing corners he might talk himself into. Such efforts are not always appreciated before, or even after the event. But the once-burned understand. One very sophisticated, polished CEO, despite meticulous preparation, allowed himself to be snared by financial analysts into speculating on a worst-possible case: one possible flat quarter after years of earnings increases. Of course the comment was purely speculative, but it caused the stock to drop several points—unfairly and unnecessarily.

What can an executive, particularly an operating manager or one isolated from the hurly-burly pressure of communicating during times of corporate upheaval and tension, learn from the experiences of others in their time of public turmoil?

- First, a manager ultimately must be his own director of intelligence, gathering information skeptically and objectively. He must insist on exact description, on accurate and detailed verification of claims and assumptions. Then he must analyze the data with intuition as well as intelligence.

- He must jettison the hubris that everything can be controlled, or at least strategically planned for. Things usually go awry. A unique cluster of misperceptions, untoward events, and mistaken decisions often produce results that no one intended and few probably even foresaw.

- Conversely, explaining everything as an accident lets managers off the hook too easily. No lessons are learned. Purposeful human decisions or responsibilities are too easily discounted.

- The best way to win a conflict may be to avoid it. Particularly in communications, prevention often succeeds where cures fail.

- Narrow, atavistic patterns and practices won't work. Changes and the pressures they produce strip away protective hypocrisies and make short-sightedness and narcissism dangerous. Nor is there safety—only danger—in relying on old habits and proven talents. As one historian cautions: those who remember the past uncritically may be the ones condemned to repeat it.

- Disciplined, intelligent intuition may be the key. Winston Churchill's life illustrates the value of this skill and of studying and understanding defeat. The British Prime Minister was said to have had a great intuitive feeling for the next lurch of history. He also accepted humiliating defeats, such as Gallipoli, as episodes natural to wielding power. But then, he was an uncommon man out of his time.

- A manager who restricts himself to linear thinking—a straight line to a solution or career success—robs himself of the subtlety, and wisdom of cyclical patterns. Nor will he be prepared for the gathering cluster of change.

- Alexander Haig sees the press assuming the ancient role of humbling the great. When a Roman emperor or general triumphantly returned to the city after a great victory, lest he be made drunk by glory and the cheers of the citizens, he was accompanied in his chariot by a dwarf/jester, who whispered into his ear, "Remember you are mortal."

In my career I have worked for profane city editors, forever infected by *Front Page* stereotypes and for wizards of ooze; for overly confident managers in the fat years, who felt they could do no wrong; and for the hand-wringers of bleaker years, who sought instant recipes for success. In the change and chaos that many companies and individuals are experiencing lies great opportunity to manage differently: more analytically and participatively, with longer-range vision and greater personal balance, and ultimately—most importantly—with communications playing a much more integrated, decisive role. But this means not looking inward or backward, but realistically reading the fever charts of corporate change, the symptoms of corporate turmoil—and then telling about it honestly.

For, just when you think everything is running smoothly, and under control . . . that one telephone call zings in, and you find yourself communicating with the whole world watching—again.

# Notes

## Chapter 1: Turbulent Times

1. V.R. Buzzota, "A Quiet Crisis in the Work Place," *The New York Times* (Sept. 4, 1985), p. A27.
2. Rafael D. Pagan, Jr, "Carrying the Fight to the Critics of Multinational Capitalism, Think and Act Politically," *Vital Speeches* (July 15, 1982), p. 589–591.
3. W. Michael Blumenthal, "Candid Reflections of a Businessman in Washington," *Fortune* (Jan. 29, 1979), p. 36–46.
4. Barbara Tuchman, *The Distant Mirror, The Calamitous Fourteenth Century* (New York: Alfred A. Knopf, 1978), pp. xiii–xiv.
5. Richard B. Madden, "A Key to Management in the 1990's," given at the *Business Week* Conference on the Future, White Plains, N.Y., April 30, 1985.
6. Harold Burson, "A Decent Respect to the Opinions of Mankind," given at the IPRA World Congress, Amsterdam, June 1985.
7. "I like people" is the most often cited reason for seeking a public relations position. "That is not a decisive grace," rebuts John Hill.
8. From various 1985 issues of *Jack O'Dwyer's Newsletter*.
9. The complete list is revealing: Financial Relations Counseling; Media Relations; Individual and Institutional Investor Communications; Banking and Financial Institution Communications; Merger and Acquisition/Takeover Communications; Proxy Solicitation and Shareholder List Analysis; Initial Public Offering and Leveraged Buy-Out Communications; Agricultural Business Communications; Marketing Communications Counseling; Sports and Recreation Marketing; Destination Marketing; Medical Products and Services Marketing; Editorial Services; Entertainment Communications; Food and Nutrition Communications; Corporate Events Production; Product Introduction Communications; Communications and Staff/Function Audits; Professional Service Firm Communications; Satellite Services and Audiovisual Productions; Industrial/Scientific/Advanced Technologies Communications; Interview, Speech, and Confrontation Training; International Economic Development Communications; College and University Relations; Public Issues/Public Policy Counseling and Communications; Japanese Business Communications; Legislative and Regulatory Monitoring and Analysis; Crisis Communications Counseling and Training; Environmental and Consumer Affairs; Corporate Design and Corporate Identity Services; Energy Affairs Communications; Employee, Labor, and Organizational Communications; Strategic Information Research/Opinion Surveys; Research and Information Services; Domestic and International Government Relations.

10. William Safire, *Before the Fall, an Inside View of the Pre-Watergate White House* (New York: Doubleday, 1975), p. 290.

11. Buzzotta, "A Quiet Crisis in the Workplace."

12. There are many differences in approach—selling products is not analyzing the gamut of public perceptions, convincing people is different than buying a way to their pocketbooks. The public, however, often confuses advertising and public relations.

13. Television will not accept this type of advertising, even accompanied by the offer to pay for equal time for an opposing view.

## Chapter 2: Bottom Line vs. Front Page

1. Howard Simons and Joseph A. Califano, Jr., eds, *The Media and Business* (New York: Vintage Books, 1979), p. ix.

2. Ibid., p. 2.

3. These comments were gathered from various writings and published speeches of Lewis H. Young, including comments at the Media and Business sessions and in "The Distorted Image" *Financial Executive* (April 1985), p. 18.

4. Some criticize the *Wall Street Journal*, noting that it had a hammerlock on information and used techniques to protect its image. It broke the story and was credited with coming clean when actually there was no choice. Also, Winan's wrong-doing, distrust, and betrayal were stressed. The *Journal* was portrayed as a trusting victim, with no questions of supervision or the paper's mistakes. Jeff and Marie Blyskal, *P.R.: How the Public Relations Industry Writes the News* (New York: William Morrow, 1985), p. 178–79.

5. A complete discussion of Behren's difficulties in getting information can be found in John C. Behrens, *The Typewriter Guerrillas: Closeups of 20 Top Investigative Reporters* (Chicago: Nelson-Hall, 1977).

6. In their book, *PR*, Jeff and Marie Blyskal cite an estimate that forty-five to fifty percent of the business news appearing in the *Wall Street Journal* on a given day was generated by press releases, merely rewrites of stories initiated by public relations people. Even worse are food pages, "a PR man's paradise," entertainment, automobile, real estate, home improvement, and living style sections. (Page 28.)

7. George E. Reedy, *Lyndon B. Johnson, A Memoir* (New York: Andrews and McMeel, 1982), p. 61.

8. This discussion is distilled from Georgie Anne Geyer, *Buying the Night Flight, The Autobiography of a Woman Foreign Correspondent* (New York: A Laurel/Merloyd Lawrence Book, 1983).

9. This discussion is drawn from Timothy Crouse, *The Boys on the Bus* (New York: Ballatine, 1972).

10. Formerly, reporters were assigned to cover a police beat or a geographic district; now, in addition, some journalists are assigned to special subjects, such as the environment or business.

11. An electronic news release—a technique that is increasingly important, but seriously debated within the news industry—is a television segment, usually produced by major public relations firms for a client and then widely distributed free to local stations. The spots carry subtle messages of corporate or national interest. Many foreign nations use them to influence U.S. public opinion on a specific issue. The reporter's voice is recorded

separate from the video track, so stations can use their own anchorperson or tailor the script to local interests. Some stations use them entirely without change; others use only portions; still others won't show them at all. Although the technique is not new, its wider use and much more sophisticated messages are raising questions of fairness in labeling sources for viewers. Proponents argue that electronic releases merely modernize the written press release—a public relations stock-in-trade for years—and that they provide national and international coverage that smaller stations cannot afford. Pro or con, both sides agree that it's an expensive, although effective, means of getting a message across.

12. Vermont Royster, "End of a Chapter," *Wall Street Journal* (March 5, 1986), p. 30.

13. Carol Loomis, "Six Handy Rules for Dealing with the Media," *Crosscurrents in Corporate Communications*, no. 14 (New York: Fortune, 1985), p. 65–68.

14. Elizabeth Podd, business editor of *The Record* in Hackensack, N.J., shared these comments with the author in conversation.

15. Walter Guzzardi, Jr., "The Politics of the Press: How to Deal with It," in *Crosscurrents in Corporate Communications*, no. 14 (New York: Fortune, 1985), p. 68–70.

16. Geyer, *Buying the Night Flight*, p. 98.

17. Oriana Fallaci, *Interview With History*, John Shepley, trans. (Boston: Houghton Mifflin, 1976), pp. 9–12.

18. Donald D. Lennox, "Reckless Reporting: The International Harvester Ordeal," in *Crosscurrents in Corporate Communications*, no. 14 (New York: Fortune, 1985), p. 60–64.

19. Lee Iacocca's comments were distilled from *Iacocca, an Autobiography* (New York: Bantam Books, 1984).

20. Ron Nessen, *It Sure Looks Different from the Inside* (New York: Playboy Press, 1978), p. 299.

21. This discussion was developed from various press reports, conversations, and Hillel Levin, *Grand Delusions, the Cosmic Career of John DeLorean* (New York: Viking Press, 1983).

22. *San Francisco Examiner* (Oct. 29, 1985), p. 1, 6.

23. *Wall Street Journal* (Aug. 21, 1985), p. 1.

24. A poll taken among journalists in the fall of 1985 reported a greater lack of credibility toward younger journalists, who were described as transients who frequently shuffled jobs and had fewer community ties. More than their older counterparts, they were likely to shrug off credibility problems as inevitable and were less inclined to fault the press for lack of public confidence. The younger journalists tended to be younger, better educated, less religious, and somewhat wealthier than the public. (*The New York Times*, Oct. 30, 1985, p. A-13.)

## Chapter 3: Planning the Unplannable

1. Meyers, in addition to his business career, is now visiting professor at Carnegie-Mellon University's Graduate School of Industrial Administration, where he discusses crisis management.

2. "Crisis Communications in American Business," prepared for Western Union by Barton-Marsteller, June 1984.

3. In addition to correspondence and conversations with Hill and Knowlton officers, infor-

mation was drawn from Richard C. Hyde's remarks to the Counselor's Section of the Public Relations Society of America in Chicago, October 9, 1979. Untitled.

4. From conversation with Phillip Fried and lecture material he has used in teaching numerous crisis management courses.

5. Material for discussion in the Tylenol section was gathered from Johnson & Johnson's public relations department, newspaper accounts in *The New York Times* and *Wall Street Journal* during both episodes, and evaluations with various communicators.

6. George Cabot Lodge discusses the absolute need for businesspeople in the future to understand and speak to the concerns of their various constituencies. He extends the Lockean concept of governing with the consent of the governed to the current business climate.

7. From lecture notes and conversation with Michael Tabriz.

## Chapter 4: Supplying Your Own Banana Peels

1. Jody Powell, President Jimmy Carter's press secretary, put it more colorfully. Speaking to the PRSA meetings in Detroit (November 1985) he said, "If one is willing to grovel before one's inferiors, it is possible to have a positive impact."

2. Ron Nessen, *It Sure Looks Different From The Inside* (New York: Playboy Press, 1978), p. 209–210.

3. Material for the Bendix phase of the Mary Cunningham–William Agee discussion was drawn from Mary Cunningham with Fran Schumer, *Powerplay, What Really Happened at Bendix* (New York: Linden Press/Simon and Schuster, 1984), and from interviews with women corporate executives, those attending the Commonwealth Club speech, and the author's listening to the WQXR broadcast.

4. The Martin Marietta phase is based on Peter F. Hartz, *Merger, the Exclusive Story of the Bendix–Martin Marietta Takeover War* (New York: William Morrow, 1985), conversations with aerospace executives in other companies, and various newspaper accounts.

5. "Lilco Is Praised by its Chairman for Storm Effort," *The New York Times* (Oct. 8, 1985), p. B4.

6. Clifford D. May, "Shoreham Plant Opponents Pressing for State Takeover of Lilco," *The New York Times* (Dec. 28, 1985), p. B5.

7. Marilyn Harris and Judith H. Dobrzynski, "Judgment Day May Be at Hand for Pierre Gousseland, Amax's Financial Crisis and His Controversial Decisions Could Cost Him His Job," *Business Week* (Sept. 30, 1985), p. 70–71.

8. Sources: the author's experience as Textron's vice president for corporate relations; her speech, "The Corporate City Room," given to the New England Section of Public Relations Society of America, Providence, April 1980, *Wall Street Journal, The New York Times, Washington Post,* and *Providence Journal* accounts; and conversation with Textron executives and communicators in CEO visibility.

9. Robert J. Schoenberg, *Geneen* (New York: Warner Books, 1985) and Harold Geneen with Alvin Moscow, *Managing* (New York: Avon, 1984) are interesting, contrasting accounts of the once-powerful CEO's departure.

10. Myron Magnet, "Is ITT Fighting Shadows—or Raiders?" *Fortune* (Nov. 11, 1985), p. 25–28.

11. Thomas J. Lueck, "Chief's Post Given Up by Gray, Technologies Names Daniell," *The New York Times* (Sept. 24, 1985), p. D1.
12. Deborah C. Wise, "Can John Sculley Clean Up the Mess at Apple?" *Business Week* (July 29, 1985), p. 70–72; "Showdown in Silicon Valley," *Newsweek* (Sept. 30, 1985), p. 46–57; Bro Uttal, "Behind the Fall," *Fortune* (Aug. 5, 1985), p. 20–24; "Apple, Part 2: The No-Nonsense Era of John Sculley," *Business Week* (Jan. 27, 1986), p. 96–97.
13. Thomas Ross, "RCA's Comeback: Communicating the Story," in *Crosscurrents in Corporate Communications,* no. 14 (New York: Fortune, 1985), p. 28–31.
14. John Eckhouse, "Apple Parties, Unveils Strategy," and John Eckhouse and Vlae Kershner, "Apple Settles Case Against Steven Jobs," *San Francisco Chronicle* (Feb. 4, 1986), p. 7.

# Chapter 5: Assets Don't Talk to Assets

1. Readers interested in the important subject of mergers—particularly the crucial issues of cultures and people—might consult some of the recent newspaper articles on which this discussion was based: Ken Wells and Carol Hymowitz, "Takeover Trauma, Gulf's Managers Find Merger into Chevron Forces Many Changes," *Wall Street Journal* (Dec. 5, 1984), p. 1, 24; Thomas F. O'Brien and Mark Russell, "Troubled Marriage: Steel Giants' Merger Brings Big Headaches, J&L and Republic Find," *Wall Street Journal* (Nov. 30, 1984), p. 1, 20; Roy J. Harris, Jr., and Damon Darlin, "GM, Hughes Face Culture Clash, Mixing Opposite Corporate Styles," *Wall Street Journal* (June 6, 1985), p. 14; Damon Darlin and Melinda Grenier Guiles, "Whose Takeover? Some GM People Feel Auto Firm, Not EDS Was the One Acquired," *Wall Street Journal* (Dec. 19, 1984), p. 1, 20; and the *Fortune* report on its 1983 Corporate Communications Seminar.
2. Richard E. Cheney, "What To Do When the Plant Blows Up and the CEO Steals Company Money and Runs Off with His or Her Secretary," a speech given before the Negative News Seminar, sponsored by the Practicing Law Institute on October 16, 1984, in New York City.
3. Raymond D'Argenio, "How To Conduct a Takeover," in *Crosscurrents in Corporate Communications,* no. 12 (New York: Fortune, 1983), p. 6–9.
4. Richard E. Cheney, "Playing Defense," in *Crosscurrents in Corporate Communications,* no. 12 (New York: Fortune, 1983), p. 1–13.
5. Martin Lipton, "Takeovers and Communication," in *Crosscurrents in Corporate Communications,* no. 12 (New York: Fortune, 1983), p. 17–23.
6. The CIGNA merger section is based on the author's observations as vice president of corporate communications, discussions with other communications and operating executives who have experienced a merger or takeover, and research in the volumes of media reports, including *The New York Times, Wall Street Journal, Fortune,* the *Philadelphia Inquirer,* and the now-defunct *Bulletin.* All quotes are from these publications, between November 1981 and June 1983.
7. Employee reactions and suggestions for communicating internally during a merger are based on insider discussions, cartoons, and merger newspapers circulated within INA and Connecticut General; and on interviews with Mr. Daniel Picard (president of Picard and Co.), Mrs. Faye Olivieri (president of Agenda), and Dr. Jan Shubert, at the time an adjunct professor in communications at the University of Michigan.

## Chapter 6: Eruptive Disasters

1. Background information on Love Canal, Hooker's role, and subsequent problems comes from *Love Canal: The Facts (1892–1982)*, Occidental Chemical Fact Line, no. 13 (Sept. 1982), balanced by conversations with chemical industry communicators, newspaper reports, and Michael Brown's *Laying Waste: The Poisoning of America by Toxic Chemicals* (New York: Pantheon Books, 1979).

2. Occidental Petroleum executives, "The Other Side of Love Canal, a Presentation Before the Financial Community Representatives from New York, Philadelphia, Boston and Hartford," in New York, July 31, 1980.

3. Eric Zuesse, "Love Canal, the Truth Seeps Out," *Reason* (Feb. 1981), p. 17–33.

4. Brown, *Laying Waste*, p. 9, 13, 25.

5. The New York Times, editorial (June 20, 1981).

6. Some charge a hidden agenda: the EPA's goal of creating massive public support for its proposed superfund.

7. *Science* (June 1981).

8. James Brooke, "Despite Toxic Waste, 350 Seek Love Canal Homes," *The New York Times* (Sept. 22, 1985), p. 54.

9. Daniel Henninger, "Keeping Cool About Environmental Disaster" (a review of Elizabeth Whelan's *Toxic Terror*), *Wall Street Journal* (Nov. 1, 1985), p. 34.

10. N.R. Kleinfield, "When Scandal Haunts the Corridors," *The New York Times* (June 16, 1985), section 3, p. 17, 26.

11. Hutton was accused of an illegal check overdraft scheme, popularly known as kiting. Fomon tried to minimize the damage by pleading Hutton guilty of 2,000 felony counts — in one fell swoop owning up to the fraudulent overdrafting.

12. James Sterngold, "The Undoing of Robert Fomon," *The New York Times* (Sept. 29, 1985), section 3, p. 1, 10, 11.

13. Douglas R. Sease, "GE's Image Makes Conviction More Jarring; Fraud Case Illustrates Difficulty of Enforcing Standards," *Wall Street Journal* (July 5, 1984), p. 4.

14. Wayne Biddle, "Lester Crown Blames the System," *The New York Times* (June 16, 1985), section 3, p. 1, 26.

15. The photograph of Lewis testifying editorializes. He is shown tight-lipped and stern with anger. The cutline reads: GD is being "badly maligned by forces beyond our control." Another picture in the same *Business Week* cover story, shows Lewis wrinkled and worried, his eyes staring as if at some awesome act. By contrast, P. Takis Veliotis, former GD executive vice president, is shown almost thoughtful and serene. *Business Week* (March 25, 1985), p. 70–72.

16. William Proxmire, "Why Military Contracting Is Corrupt: Cleaning Up Procurement," *The New York Times* (Dec. 15, 1985), section 3, p. 3.

17. "General Dynamics Under Fire, as the Circle Widens, Indictment May Be Underway," *Business Week* (March 25, 1985), p. 70–76.

18. The detail for airline crisis planning was developed in conversation with Jerry Full, formerly a crisis manager with major airlines.

19. The most important sources for the section on differences in cultural reactions to airline crashes were: Susan Chera, "JAL's Post-Crash Troubles," *The New York Times* (Nov. 8, 1985), p. D. 1: and John J. Nance, *Blind Trust, How Deregulation Has Jeopardized Airline Safety and What You Can Do About It.* (New York: William Morrow, 1986).

20. This material was distilled from extensive coverage by the *Wall Street Journal* and *The New York Times*, plus Susan and Dawson Perry, *Nightmare: Women and the Dalkon Shield* (New York: MacMillan, 1985).

21. Bhopal has been so extensively covered that only major sources will be noted. Also, this section reflects the understandably great attention the tragedy has attracted among communicators, who continue to discuss it from many angles. Insights into Warren Anderson come from those who know him, reputation, and from Stuart Diamond, "Warren Anderson: A Public Crisis, a Personal Ordeal," *The New York Times* (May 19, 1985), section 3, p. 1, 8, 9.

22. *The New York Times* (Aug. 13, 1985) p. B9.

23. "Bhopal Has Americans Demanding the 'Right to Know'," *Business Week* (Feb. 18, 1985), p. 36–37.

24. Cathy Trost, "OSHA Plans To Fine Carbide $1.4 Million. Alleges Violation at West Va. Plant," *Wall Street Journal* (April 2, 1986), p. 2.

## Chapter 7: Winning with Communications

1. "Bank of Boston: A Public Relations Nightmare," *Business Week* (March 4, 1985), p. 78.

2. The bank pleaded guilty to charges of failing to report $1.2 billion worth of international cash transactions. *Ibid.*

3. The bank's closing sent tremors through world financial markets: the dollar dropped and gold soared. Seventy other Ohio thrift institutions closed temporarily. General source: James Ring Adams, "How Ohio's Home State Beat the Examiners," *Wall Street Journal* (Sept. 15, 1985), p. 5.

4. B of A is an important symbol in the Bay Area. Its phoenix-like rise to a banking giant symbolized San Francisco's recovery from the 1906 earthquake and fire. Its towering black stone headquarters, now sold, is an important part of the city's skyline.

5. Ronald E. Rhody, "Nobody Told Me It'd Be Like This," a Bank of America Speech Reprint of remarks made at the Public Relations Roundtable, San Francisco, May 28, 1985. For further analysis on the weakness of detailed plans under crisis, see the discussion of Tylenol in chapter 3.

6. Fredrick Koenig, "Rumors That Follow the Sun," *Across the Board* (Feb. 1985), p. 25–30.

7. Information gathered from conversations with American Banking Association representatives, bankers, and regulators. Instructions to individual banks are contained in a press kit: "Priority: The Voluntary Effort, Banker Commitment to Consumer Concerns."

8. John Bussey, "Wise Guys—and Newspapers—Still Bedevil P&G About Its Infamous Corporate Logo," *Wall Street Journal* (May 29, 1985), p. 21.

9. Robert A. Sigafoos, *Absolutely Positively Overnight: The Story of Federal Express* (New York: A Mentor Book from New American Library, 1983), p. 223.

10. In addition to a conversation with Richard Weiner, material was gathered from: *Jack O'Dwyer's Newsletter* (Dec. 14, 1983), p. 1; *PR News*, Case Study no. 1963; and *Burrelle's Clipping Analyst* (July 1984).

11. N.R. Kleinfield, "Coleco Moves out of the Cabbage Patch," *The New York Times* (July 21, 1985), p. F4.

12. The Puna case reflects my own fifteen-year association with Amfac, first as consultant, now as a member of the board of directors; conversations with Henry A. Walker, Jr.

(CEO during the Puna closing), Harry Matte (senior vice president of Corporate Communications), and Robert H. Ozaki (vice president for public affairs, based in Honolulu); the transcript of the press conference to announce the closing; various newspaper articles from the *Honolulu Bulletin* and *Star Advertiser*; and Silver Anvil Winner abstracts from 1982 and 1983.

## Chapter 8: Understanding the Janus Manager

1. Janus is an ancient Roman deity who presided over doors and gates, and beginnings and endings. He was commonly represented with two faces looking in opposite directions. Translated to communications, Janus represents the corporate officer who, to be effective, must face outward to the world, yet inward to his peers and the business.
2. Edward L. Bernays, *Biography of an Idea: Memoirs of PR Counsel* (New York: Simon and Schuster, 1965), p. 374.
3. John W. Hill wrote two books. The first, *Corporate Public Relations, Arm of Modern Management* (New York: Harper & Brothers, 1958), details the concept—more valid today than when Hill wrote—that communications must be in the matrix of its times, meeting needs. The second work is somewhat autobiographical; *The Making of a Public Relations Man* (New York: David McKay, 1963).
4. Kepone is an unremembered historical footnote today. In 1975, tremors, headaches, and sterility were reported by residents in Virginia. Allied Chemical Company (now Allied Signal) was reported dumping the insecticide into the James River. Allied reacted by investing heavily in antipollution and safety equipment. The malaise disappeared. The kepone incident illustrates, once again, a very public, costly problem that could have been headed off by thinking publicly.
5. Readers interested in the startling transformations in United Fruit's public relations, which in many ways tracking corporate communications itself, are directed to McCann's book, *An American Company, The Tragedy of United Fruit* (New York: Crown, 1976).
6. Prince Gregori Alexsandrovich Potemkin, a Russian statesman and a favorite of Catherine the Great, constructed sham villages along the banks of the Dneiper River. He marshaled the peasantry to create the illusion of progress. Although these facades may have totally impressed foreign diplomats, Catherine understood that behind the sham was some sound prosperity and progress.
7. Men want to endow women with all the noble, good, and kind instincts that many men wish they could display openly in corporate life. When a woman not only eschews this basically peripheral role but also demonstrates greater realism than her male colleagues toward the hard-knuckled world outside the corporation, she is in for trouble—no matter how capable she is.
8. Ronald E. Rhody, "Public Relations for the CEO," Bank of America Reprint of remarks to the Young Presidents Organization, Palo Alto, Ca., September 20, 1984.
9. Circumscribed *Literary Digest*-type thinking is dangerous and misleading. Poll only those who have telephones, as *Literary Digest* did in 1932, and of course Herbert Hoover will be predicted to win the presidency. That's akin to taking a poll at a private eating club, the country club, or the Business Roundtable.

10. These activities traditionally translate into: employee and financial communications; media, government, and community relations; public information; external publications; contributions; product publicity; corporate advertising (usually image-oriented rather than product); and issues management.

# Bibliography

## Books

James Baar, *The Great Free Enterprise Gambit* (Boston: Houghton Mifflin, 1980).

Loren Baritz, *A History of How American Culture Led Us into Vietnam and Made Us Fight the Way We Did* (New York: William Morrow, 1985).

Marvin Barrett and Zachary Sklar, *The Eye of the Storm* (New York: Lippincott and Crowell, 1980).

John C. Behrens, *The Typewriter Guerrillas, Closeups of 20 Top Investigative Reporters* (Chicago: Nelson-Hall, 1977).

Daniel Bell, *The Coming of Post-Industrial Society, Adventure in Social Forecasting* (New York: Basic Books, 1973).

Edward L. Bernays, *Biography of an Idea: Memoirs of P.R. Counsel* (New York: Simon & Schuster, 1965).

Carl Bernstein and Bob Woodward, *All the President's Men* (New York: Simon & Schuster, 1974).

Jeff and Marie Blyska, *PR, How the Public Relations Industry Writes the News* (New York: William Morrow, 1985).

Heinrich Böll, *The Lost Honor of Katharina Blum* (New York: McGraw-Hill, 1975).

Arnaud de Borchgrave and Robert Moss, *The Spike* (New York: Avon, 1980).

Paul Brodeur, *Outrageous Misconduct, the Asbestos Industry on Trial* (New York: Pantheon, 1985).

Michael Brown, *Laying Waste: The Poisoning of America by Toxic Chemicals* (New York: Pantheon, 1979).

Timothy Crouse, *The Boys on the Bus* (New York: Ballantine, 1972).

Mary Cunningham with Fran Schumer, *Powerplay, What Really Happened at Bendix* (New York: Linden Press/Simon & Schuster, 1984).

Peter Drucker, *Innovation and Entrepreneurship, Practice and Principles* (New York: Harper & Row, 1985).

Marilyn Ferguson, *The Aquarian Conspiracy, Personal and Social Transformation in the 1980's* (Los Angeles: J.P. Tarcher, 1980).

Stephen Fox, *A History of American Advertising and Its Creators* (New York: Vintage, 1984).

Hugh Gregory Gallagher, *FDR's Splendid Deception* (New York: Dodd, Mead, 1985).

Joel Garreau, *The Nine Nations of North America* (Boston: Houghton Mifflin, 1981).

Harold Geneen with Alvin Moscow, *Managing* (New York: Avon, 1984).

Georgie Anne Geyer, *Buying the Night Flight, the Autobiography of a Woman Foreign Correspondent* (New York: A LaVrel/Merloyd Lawrence Book, 1983).

Eli Ginzberg and George Vojta, *Beyond Human Scale, the Large Corporations at Risk* (New York: Basic Books, 1985).

Tom Goldstein, *The News at Any Cost, How Journalists Compromise Their Ethics to Shape the News* (New York: Simon & Schuster, 1985).

Mark Green and Robert Massie, Jr., eds., *The Big Business Reader, Essays on Corporate America* (New York: The Pilgrim Press, 1980).

Andrew S. Grove, *High Output Management,* (New York: Random House, 1983).

Alexander M. Haig, Jr., *Caveat: Realism, Reagan and Foreign Policy* (New York: Macmillan, 1984).

Peter F. Hartz, *Merger, the Exclusive Story of the Bendix—Martin Marietta Takeover War* (New York: William Morrow, 1985).

John W. Hill, *Corporate Public Relations, Arm of Modern Management* (New York: Harper & Brothers, 1958).

————, *The Making of a Public Relations Man* (New York: David McKay, 1963).

Lee Iacocca with William Novak, *Iacocca, an Autobiography* (New York: Bantam Books, 1984).

Paul Johnson, *Modern Times, the World from the Twenties to the Eighties* (New York: Harper & Row, 1983).

Rosabeth Moss Kanter, *The Change Masters, Innovation and Entrepreneurship in the American Corporation* (New York: Simon & Schuster, 1983).

Stanley Karnow, *Vietnam: A History, the First Complete Account of the Vietnam War* (New York: Viking Press, 1983).

Charles P. Kindleberger, *Maniacs, Panics and Crashes, a History of Financial Crisis* (New York: Basic Books, 1978).

Hillel Levin, *Grand Delusions, the Cosmic Career of John DeLorean* (New York: Viking Press, 1983).

Steven Levy, *Hackers, Heroes of the Computer Revolution* (Garden City: Anchor Press/Doubleday, 1984).

Royal Little, *How to Lose $100,000,000 and Other Valuable Advice* (Boston: Little, Brown, 1979).

George C. Lodge, *The New American Ideology* (New York: Alfred A. Knopf, 1975).

————, *The American Disease* (New York: Alfred A. Knopf, 1984).

Richard Louv, *America II* (New York: Viking Penguin, 1973).

Tom Mangold and John Penycate, *The Tunnels of CuChi* (New York: Random House, 1985).

Rollo May, *The Courage to Create* (New York: W.W. Norton, 1975).

Martin Mayer, *The Money Bazaars, Understanding the Banking Revolution Around Us* (New York: A Mentor Book, New American Library, 1984).

Thomas McCann, *An American Company, the Tragedy of United Fruit* (New York: Crown, 1976).

David McClintock, *Indecent Exposure, a True Story of Hollywood and Wall Street* (New York: Dell, 1982).

Lance Morrow, *The Chief, a Memoir of Fathers and Sons* (New York: Random House, 1984).

John J. Nance, *Blind Trust, How Deregulation Has Jeopardized Airline Safety and What You Can Do About It* (New York: William Morrow, 1986).

Ron Nessen, *It Sure Looks Different from the Inside* (New York: Playboy Press, 1978).

Michael Novak, *The Spirit of Democratic Capitalism* (New York: American Enterprise Institute/Simon & Schuster, 1982).

C. Northcote Parkinson and Nigel Rowe, *Communicate, Parkinson's Formula for Business Survival* (Englewood Cliffs, N.J.: Prentice-Hall, 1978).

C. Northcote Parkinson, *Big Business* (Boston: Little, Brown, 1974).

M. Scott Peck, M.D., *People of the Lie, the Hope for Healing Human Evil* (New York: Simon & Schuster, 1983).

*The People and the Press* (A Times-Mirror Investigation of Public Attitudes Toward the News Media Conducted by the Gallup Organization) (Los Angeles: *Times-Mirror*, 1986).

Susan and Dawson Perry, *Nightmare, Women and the Dalkon Shield* (New York: Macmillan, 1985).

Tom Peters and Nancy Austin, *A Passion for Excellence, the Leadership Difference* (New York: Random House, 1985).

Thomas J. Peters and Robert H. Waterman, Jr., *In Search of Excellence, Lessons from America's Best-Run Companies* (New York: Harper & Row, 1982).

Norman Polmar and Thomas B. Allen, *Rickover* (New York: Simon & Schuster, 1982).

John Clark Pratt, *Vietnam Voices, Perspectives on the War Years, 1941–1942* (New York: Penguin, 1984).

Dan Rather with Mickey Herskowitz, *The Camera Never Blinks, Adventures of a T.V. Journalist* (New York: Ballantine, 1977).

George E. Reedy, *Lyndon B. Johnson, a Memoir* (New York: Andrews and McMeel, 1982).

———, *The Twilight of the Presidency* (New York: A Mentor Book, New American Library, 1970).

William Safire, *Before the Fact, an Inside View of the Pre-Watergate White House* (New York: Doubleday, 1975).

Stephen Salsbury, *No Way to Run a Railroad, the Untold Story of the Penn Central Crisis* (New York: McGraw-Hill, 1982).

Robert J. Schoenberg, *Geneen* (New York: Warner, 1985).

Robert A. Sigafoos, *Absolutely Positively Overnight, the Story of Federal Express* (New York: A Mentor Book, New American Library, 1983).

Howard Simons and Joseph A. Califano, Jr., eds., *The Media and Business* (New York: Vintage, 1979).

Sun Tzu, *The Art of War*, Samuel B. Griffith, trans. (London: Oxford University Press, 1963).

Alvin Toffler, *Previews and Premises* (New York: William Morrow, 1983).

Barbara W. Tuchman, *A Distant Mirror, the Calamitous Fourteenth Century* (New York: Alfred A. Knopf, 1978).

I.M. Vested, *The Confidential Memos of I.M. Vested* (New York: Harcourt Brace Jovanovitch, 1981).

Mike Wallace and Gary Paul Gates, *Close Encounters, Mike Wallace's Own Story* (New York: William Morrow, 1984).

Sloan Wilson, *The Man in the Gray Flannel Suit* (New York: Simon & Schuster, 1955).

## Publications

*Business Week*

*Encounter*

*Fortune*

*Fortune Crosscurrents of Corporate Communications*

*Forbes*

*The Guardian*

*Harvard Business Review*

*Honolulu Star-Advertiser*

*New Republic*

*The New York Times*

*Philadelphia Bulletin* (defunct)

*Philadelphia Inquirer*

*The Record* (Hackensack, N.J.)

*San Francisco Chronicle*

*Wall Street Journal*

## Speeches

Chester Burger, (no title), the Vern C. Schranz Distinguished Lectureship in Public Relations at Ball State University, Muncie, Indiana, November 10, 1983.

Harold Burson, "A Decent Respect to the Opinions of Mankind," presented at the IPRA World Congress, Amsterdam, June 1985.

Richard E. Cheney, "What to Do When the Plant Blows Up and the CEO Steals Company Money and Runs Off with His or Her Secretary," presented at the Negative News Seminar, Practicing Law Institute, New York, October 16, 1984.

Robert L. Dilenschneider and Richard C. Hyde, "Crisis Communications, Planning the Unplanned," published by Hill and Knowlton, Inc.

Richard C. Hyde, (no title), presented at the Counselor's Section of the Public Relations Society of America, Chicago, October 9, 1979.

Richard B. Madden, "A Key to Management in the 1990's," presented at the *Business Week* Conference on the Future, White Plains, New York, April 30, 1985.

Saul P. Steinberg, "Maximizing Investment Decisions," presented at the Wharton School, University of Pennsylvania, March 28, 1984.

Saul P. Steinberg, "Mergers and Acquisitions: Realities of a Drastically Changing Marketplace," presented at the Wharton School, University of Pennsylvania, February 19, 1985.

# Index

# About the Author

M ARION K. Pinsdorf uniquely combines experience as a journalist, corporate officer and director with a Ph.D. in economic history. Dr. Pinsdorf is a member of Amfac's Board of Directors, an adjunct professor at Brown University, and a partner of a New York–based consulting firm. Previously, the author was a vice president of Hill and Knowlton, of Textron while G. William Miller served in two U.S. Presidential appointments, and of INA during its merger with Connecticut General into CIGNA. Dr. Pinsdorf's counsel in this book has been battle-tested over more than twenty years in the trenches of communications counseling and managing public crises.

**Marion K. Pinsdorf,** an experienced journalist, corporate executive, and communications counselor, is a member of Amfac Inc.'s Board of Directors, a partner of Chester Burger and Co., and an adjunct professor at Brown University.